Gen. Robert E. Lee

LIVING CONFEDERATE PRINCIPLES
A Heritage For All Time

by Lloyd Tilghman Everett
Washington Camp, No. 305
Sons of Confederate Veterans

with
Appendices

THE CONFEDERATE
REPRINT COMPANY
☆   ☆   ☆   ☆
WWW.CONFEDERATEREPRINT.COM

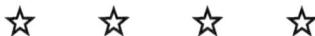

Living Confederate Principles
A Heritage For All Time
by Lloyd Tilghman Everett

Originally Published in 1917
by Yexid Publishing Company
Ballston, Virginia

Reprint Edition © 2016
The Confederate Reprint Company
Post Office Box 2027
Toccoa, Georgia 30577
www.confederatereprint.com

Cover and Interior Design by
Magnolia Graphic Design
www.magnoliagrapicdesign.com

ISBN-13: 978-1945848032
ISBN-10: 1945848030

CHAPTER ONE

☆ ☆ ☆ ☆

We often hear it said that the glory of the Confederate soldier is imperishable and immortal; that his valor and devotion to duty have won for him a name and a fame that shall never die. That is true. History shows us no equal to the splendid blend of physical and moral courage and long sustained fortitude of the half starved legions of Lee – certainly no superior. And while, to use a homely phrase, every tub must stand upon its own bottom – while each man must win for himself, by his own worth, his standing in the community – yet I prize as a priceless treasure the proud fact that I am the son of a Confederate soldier. Nor is this merely a matter of pride or of accidental honor to me. It is a very real incentive to look well to my own course and conduct in order that I may hand on untarnished, the shining legacy that was bequeathed to me.

"Duty is the sublimest word in the English language," is a maxim that has been widely credited to our peerless Lee, although incorrectly so according to respectable authority.[1] But, in any event, the sentiment is well worthy of General Lee, whose own life, public and private, was a superb illustration of the truth of the sublime epigram. And so, unswerving and unfaltering devotion to duty is the glorious heritage which we Sons of Confederate Veterans, *as* sons of Confederate veterans, have acquired by reason of our lineage.

But it is not of the courage, valor and endurance of the Confederate soldier that I wish particularly to speak on this occasion. Those cardinal virtues of Dixie's defenders have been extolled a thousand times over by tongues more fluent than mine. Nor is it my purpose to vindicate the course of the peoples of the Southern States in asserting, and striving at all costs to maintain

---

1. The purported letter of Gen. Lee containing the expression is found in Dr. J. Wm. Jones' *Personal Reminiscences, Anecdotes and Letters of Gen. Robt. E. Lee*, 1875, p. 133. Capt. James Power Smith, of the Southern Historical Society, advises me that Professor Graves, of the University of Virginia, has examined the question in an Address before the Bar Association of Virginia, and reached the conclusion that the letter was not written by General Lee; also, that the Publishing Committee of the Society concurs in this conclusion. – L.T.E.

their independence under the exigencies of the particular crisis of 1860-61. The world is already coming to know, as we have always known, that we need no such vindication – that our open record is its own vindication.

No, it is another phase of what we may call the Confederate subject which I wish here to discuss – a phase which, it seems to me, has been too little featured and, I fear, too little recognized, even by our own chroniclers and advocates. And yet, to my mind, upon the general recognition of it depends the true progress of our own people; nay, of free government, and hence of civilization itself. And that phase or aspect of the general subject is this: *The absolute soundness of the principles upon which the Southern Confederacy was bottomed;* not merely the rightfulness of our stand for political independence under the peculiar circumstances of that time, but the everlasting verity of the political and institutional ideals underlying our action – ideals vital and essential to all ages and climes as a goal toward which to press, if the world is to have true *liberty with progress.*

For our Confederate war – our second war for independence, as Stonewall Jackson called it[2]

---

2. Gen. Jackson's farewell address to the "Stonewall Brigade," Oct. 4, 1861: John Esten Cooke's *Stonewall Jackson: A Military Biography*, 1876, p. 856.

– was not a mere abortive revolution. We of the Southern States stood for great and fundamental principles of government; principles that meant, *and that still mean* much for the advancement of free institutions and of human happiness.

And, just as the valor of the Confederate soldier and the untold heroism of the Confederate woman are immortal, so, with this larger view of the subject in mind, I take a theme for consideration here, and name it:

Living Confederate Principles:
A Heritage for all Time.

CHAPTER TWO

☆ ☆ ☆ ☆

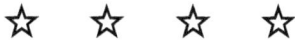

The present is a time of peace and good will, of broad and tolerant sentiment, of generous breadth of view; in a word, it is an era of good feeling between the various sections of these United States.

Just now there is rolling past us the semi-centenary of the War for Southern Independence – the "Civil War" – the War between the States or the sections – the "War of the Rebellion" (whether by the North or the South, we need not here inquire) – call it what one will; everyone knows to what we here refer; that mighty clash of arms which to many of us is still most commonly referred to as, simply, The War. On every hand, to judge from the newspapers, are daily evidences of amity and cordiality between the Grey and the Blue; of honor accorded brave men by brave men. And in July, 1913, at Gettysburg, there was formally and finally buried – let us see, was it the twenty-seventh time, or the hundred and twenty-seventh time, since the war with Spain? – "the last vestige of sectionalism." And when I see and hear all this, I am glad. For then I may claim the right to a respectful hearing on my chosen theme, even though certain views I hold regarding The War, its causes, its conduct and its consequences, may differ widely from those prevalent in the North, and even from those sometimes found in the South.

Nor is this era of good feeling confined to America. Just now a son of Virginia and of a Confederate veteran sits in the White House, and a grandson of Virginia is the premier of the cabinet. From these two men of Southern stock now at the helm of the ship of state, has gone forth to all the world the message from this mighty nation, Peace on earth, good will to men; not good will to men on earth from God in Heaven, as on that Christmas morn nineteen centuries ago, but peace on earth from men to men – in truth, a clarion call from a strong nation to the other nations of the earth, strong and weak alike; a call to these other nations to recognize as never before the brotherhood of man under the Fatherhood of God, as it is sometimes expressed. Under the Bryan Peace plan, if adopted, a long step forward will have been taken toward that happy era when "they shall beat their swords into plow-shares, and their spears into pruning hooks; nation shall not lift up sword against nation, neither shall they learn war any more."[1]

This means a turning from the forum of force to the rule of reason; a substitution of calm argument or impartial arbitration for the dread arbitrament of war. Yea, veterans and descendants of the Grey, it means a turning from the principles and practices of Lincoln and the North; it means the coming triumph of the underlying principles of the Confederate States of America.

I know that it is often said that the Southern States appealed to the sword in their controversy with the Northern States. I am here to challenge that allegation; to absolutely deny its truth. And I can prove my contention from the record, and prove it to the verge of demonstration. That record shows that the South did not choose the arbitrament of the sword; it does show that *she resorted to secession as the last hope of* PEACE WITH HONOR.

Ours is pre-eminently a race of peace and progress through the channels of self-government. The history of our ancestors for a thousand years and more will sustain the truth of this claim. True, it is a history of internecine war, of-

---

1. The Bible, Isaiah ii, 4.

ten, but largely so because it is the life story of men, and of many generations of men, who prized peace and order so highly that they were ever ready, if need be, to fight for it. Magna Charta, the Bill of Rights, the Petition of Right, the Revolution of 1688, the Act of Settlement – these are some of the monuments that mark the achievements of this orderly yet militant race. And these men laid the corner-stone of their structure in local self-government, as the truest safeguard for an oppressed minority, and thus the surest bulwark for political liberty itself. Yes, local self-government, or home rule, is of the very warp and woof of our institutions.

These salutary political principles, these racial characteristics, were transplanted also to the kindly soil of the New World when a greater Britain was planted here.

It was in support of these principles that our Revolutionary sires protested against the unconstitutional stamp acts and similar taxation measures of England oppressive of the American minority, in the efforts of the mother country to recuperate for the expenses of the French and Indian war. At first, they sought a peaceable remedy in the form of remonstrances, resolutions and the like. When they found that these availed them not, they then reluctantly accepted the gauge of battle flung in their faces by their haughty oppressors across the seas. Even after actual war was raging, these American patriots of British stock still indulged the fatuous dream of an unbroken British union, and sought to wage their fight under the British crown and, as nearly as possible, under the British flag.[2] As himself afterward declared, George Washington, when he took command of the rebel forces under authority from the Continental Congress, *"abhorred the idea of independence."*[3]

But the logic of events soon brought forth the instrument officially entitled "The unanimous Declaration of the thirteen united States of America."[4] (And, by the way, Declaration is written with a big *D*, united States with a little *u* and a capital *S*.) This immortal declaration laid down the fundamental doctrine that:

"Governments are instituted among men, deriving their just powers from the consent of the

2. "It is related that the flag which was raised at Cambridge, January 2, 1776, by Washington, was composed of thirteen red and white stripes, with the crosses of St. George and St. Andrew emblazoned on the blue canton in place of the stars." – Brown & Strauss' *Dictionary of American Politics*, article "Flag of the United States."

3. A.H. Stephens' *History of the United States*, p. 225.

4. Revised Statutes of the United States, 1878, copy of the Declaration of Independence, certified by Ferdinand Jefferson, official custodian, or "Keeper of the Rolls at the Department of State."

governed; that, whenever any form of government becomes destructive of these ends, it is the right of the people to alter or to abolish it, and to institute a new government, laying its foundation on such principles, and organizing its powers in such form, as to them shall seem most likely to effect their safety and happiness."

This, our first war for independence, was successful. About the close of it these thirteen independent republics formed a closer union among themselves, under what was known as the Articles of Confederation. This becoming unsatisfactory after a very few years, most of the constituent States seceded (which at the time was denounced by a few as unconstitutional and a breach of faith[5]), and these seceding States, eleven in number, formed a new union under the Federal Constitution that was framed in 1787 and went into operation between these eleven States March 4, 1789. Afterward the two remaining States of

---

5. See, for instance, action of the convention of North Carolina which refused to accede to the Federal Constitution of 1787, adopting by a large majority a resolution recommending to the Legislature to pass similar impost laws to those to be passed by the Congress under the Constitution "and appropriate the money arising therefrom to the use of Congress"; i.e., thus refusing to recognize the secession of the ratifying States from the old Confederation. Elliot's *Debates*, Vol. IV., p. 251.

the old union, North Carolina and Rhode Island, also acceded to the new instrument.

As is well known, this new Union was regarded with great jealousy, and scrutinized very closely by a number of the Continental fathers, the immortal Patrick Henry, the firebrand of the Revolution, and George Mason, author of the great Bill of Rights of Virginia, among the number. As just seen, political independence from the despotic central power of Britain had been gained by the assertion and maintenance of the right to change oppressive governments. But this struggle was won by force of arms and at the cost of much bloodshed; and the principle of the right to alter oppressive governments thus asserted in the Declaration of Independence might be construed, it was feared, to mean merely the right of revolution, and so the people of some of the United States, if thereafter oppressed by the central Government to be created under the new Constitution, might be left the right of separation, in self-defense, only by force of arms. And thus we would have progressed no whither in our supposed upward and onward march in the path of just and orderly self-government. Wherefore, several of the States – Virginia, New York and Rhode Island – in acceding to the new Constitution, expressly reserved the right to peaceably withdraw or secede, should they thereafter find it necessary to their happiness to do so.[6]

This was an important advance in self-government, and a further safeguard for the minority. The protection of the minority, be it remembered, was a primary object in the framing of the Federal Constitution, as stated at the time by James Madison, who is called the Father of the Constitution. In the Virginian convention that ratified the Constitution of the United States, delegate James Madison declared:

"But, on a candid examination of history, we shall find that turbulence, violence and abuse of power by the majority trampling on the rights of the minority, have produced factions and commotions which, in republics, have more frequently than any other cause produced despotism. . . . If we consider the peculiar situation of the United States, and what are the sources of that diversity of sentiment which pervades its [sic] inhabitants, we shall find great danger to fear that the same causes may terminate here in the same fatal effects which they produced in those republics. This danger ought to be wisely guarded against."[7]

---

6. See Elliot's *Debates*, Vol. I., pp. 327, 327-9, 334-5; Stephens' *History of the United States*, pp. 339-40, 347-50, 358-61.

7. Elliot's *Debates*, Vol. III., p. 87.

Madison advocated the adoption of the Constitution as affording the needed protection to the minority.

Remember that: the Constitution of the United States was framed and adopted, the Union of the States thereunder was formed, for the *peaceable* protection of the *minority* against the oppressions of the majority. And mark this: it was proposed by some to embody in the Constitution a power to coerce States that might refuse to obey the laws of Congress. Madison (still the father of the Constitution) said that this would mean war, and the proposal was voted down.[8]

Well, time went on. Sectional differences and jealousies speedily developed between the Southern and the Northern States. Under Jefferson, a Southern President, the great trans-Mississippi territory of Louisiana was bought from Napoleon, in 1803; and thereby the area of the United States was approximately doubled. New England thought that this would strengthen the South at the expense of the North. Accordingly, New England threatened secession.[9]

---

8. *Ib.*, Vol. V., pp. 127-8, 140.

9. McMaster's *Hist. People of the United States,* Vol. III., p. 42; 2 Hy. Adams' *History of the United States*, 160 et seq.; Powell's *Nullification and Secession in the United States*, chap. 3.

New England was at this time a commercial or sea-faring country, and had as yet few manufactures. The Embargo law of Jefferson's second administration was unpopular in this sea-trading New England, and again loud mutterings of secessionist purposes were heard up there.[10] The State of Louisiana was admitted in 1812, despite the celebrated threat of Josiah Quincy, of Massachusetts, on the floor of Congress in 1811, that such admission of a new Southern State from a part of the Louisiana purchase would constitute adequate cause for secession by some of the Northern States, "amicably if they can, violently if they must."[11]

But conditions soon changed. The war of 1812 cut us off from Europe, whence we had theretofore obtained most of our manufactured goods; and New England, her sea-trade interrupted by the war, with commendable energy and enterprise now began to manufacture. During this war the famous Hartford Convention, of New England, met, with a large sized list toward secession.[12] After the war New England and the

---

10. McMaster, Vol. III., chap. 19; 4 Hy. Adams, p. 407, 431.

11. *Congressional Speeches of Josiah Quincy*, edited by his son, Edmund Quincy (1874), p. 196.

12. See a host of authorities, including Stephens' *History of the United States*, p. 419.

North generally began to find the Union a good thing for them; it furnished a free market – the Southern States – for buying the manufacturers' raw materials; it furnished a "protected" market – still largely the Southern States – for selling the manufactured goods.

But New England and the rest of the North were still painfully jealous of new Southern and Western or Southwestern States. They opposed the admission of Missouri, 1819, and now first raised seriously the question of Negro slavery as a sectional issue. Thomas Jefferson was himself, like many other Southerners, in favor of the abolition of slavery – a peaceable abolition. But he could see further into the future than could most men. So now, when this Missouri-slavery issue was raised by New England and the North, for the purpose of keeping the new lands of the West for themselves as against the South, the aged Jefferson wrote that it roused him as a fire-bell in the night, and portended a disastrous sectional struggle.[13]

---

13. Jefferson to Holmes, April 22, 1820, *The Writings of Thomas Jefferson* (1829), Vol. IV., pp. 323-4; also, in *Jefferson's Complete Works*, Vol. VI., p. 159, as cited in Stephens' *History of the United States,* p. 431.

CHAPTER THREE

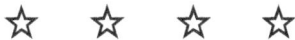

☆ ☆ ☆ ☆

To return to the tariff: The tariff question, as a serious sectional issue, first came to a head about 1830. Having once gotten hold of the nursing bottle of "protection," so called, in 1816 and 1820, New England and the North cried ever for more. The tariff of 1820 was followed by that of 1824, and that in turn by the "tariff of abominations" in 1828. These were sectional measures, and the South felt herself being oppressed and impoverished by the combined Northern and North-western majority. The tariff act of 1832 was of the same stripe as its predecessors. Out of this situation came the Nullification crisis of 1830-33.

Early in 1830 occurred the memorable debate in the Senate of the United States between Robert Y. Hayne, of South Carolina, and Daniel Webster, of Massachusetts. Just three years later, early in 1833, a similar debate took place between the same Mr. Webster on one side and, on the other side, Hayne's successor in the Senate, the immortal John C. Calhoun. Hayne and Calhoun were the champions of the South in the pending sectional controversy; Webster, of the North. In these debates Webster is said to have "shotted every gun" that was fired for the North in the great War of thirty years later.[1] If this be so, careful attention is due to this Titans' war, this battle of the forensic giants, and to the great constitutional and institutional arguments then advanced.

The immediate issue was the tariff. The Southern States, and especially South Carolina, contended that the existing tariff laws were devised for *protecting* Northern manufacturers, and so imposed a sectional burden upon the agricultural South; they contended, further, that there was no warrant for anything more than a *revenue* tariff; that a tariff for "protection," as it is called, was utterly unconstitutional.

Whether the South was correct on these two points; viz: the injurious effects of a "protective" tariff at that time, upon the South, and the unconstitutionality of such a tariff ,with these two

---

1. Quoted from memory; author or origin not now recalled.

222

questions we are not here concerned. But from this starting point the debates ranged out and covered the other two questions which do here concern us. And these are: first, How are disputed questions of constitutionality, arising between States, or groups of States, in the Union, to be determined?; second, The nature of the Union, whether a union of States as States, or of the American people in one aggregate mass?

To take these up briefly, in inverse order to that just given: Calhoun introduced in the Senate a series of resolutions, three in number, which are well worth the careful study of every student of republican institutions, every lover of human freedom. These resolutions recited the strictly federal character, under the Constitution of 1787-89, of the Union of American States; with the resultant right, to the States, "of judging, in the last resort, as to the extent of the powers delegated" to the central Government and, consequently, of those reserved to the several States, and that action by the central Government based upon the contrary assumption must inevitably tend to undue consolidation and to "the loss of liberty itself."[2]

Webster vehemently attacked these resolutions. His argument may be thus epitomized, large-

2. Jenkins' *Calhoun*, pp. 248-9.

ly in his own words: How can any man get over the words of the preamble to the Constitution itself, *"We the people* of the United States . . . do ordain and establish this constitution"?; that these words forbid the turning of the instrument into a mere compact between sovereign States; that, in framing and putting into operation the Constitution of the United States, "a change had been made from a *confederacy* of States to a different system, . . . a *constitution* for a national government"; that "accession, as a word applied to political associations, implies coming into a league treaty or *confederacy,* by one hitherto a stranger to it"; that, "in establishing the present government," (i.e., the Government of the United States as it stood in Webster's time) the "people of the United States . . . do not say that they *accede* to a *league,* but they declare that they *ordain and establish a constitution,* . . . some of them employing the . . . words 'assented to' and 'adopted,' but all of them 'ratifying'"; that "the constitution of the United States is *not* a league, confederacy or *compact* between the people of the several States in their sovereign capacities"; that "THE NATURAL CONVERSE OF ACCESSION IS SECESSION."[3]

---

18. See the writer's monograph, "A Titans' War," chap. 34.

Note the several test words here: *confederacy, constitution, national, compact* and ACCEDE.

As to every one of them Webster was wrong, as may be shown from the debates and official documents accompanying and preceding the framing and adoption of the Federal Constitution. We have not the time to examine fully into all these test words here; for a fairly full compilation or tabulation of the data bearing on them, see the subjoined note.[4] To one or two of these words let us devote a few sentences.

First, then, as to the phrase, "We the people of the United States." The preamble to the Federal Constitution does use this expression. But Article VII of the instrument itself provides that "The ratification of the conventions of nine *States* shall be sufficient for the establishment of

---

4. *Accede*, some 58 times in Elliot's *Debates*; *compact* or *contract*, over 30 times, *ibid.*; *confederacy, confederated republic, federal* (under the new Constitution, or in the Federal Convention of 1787), some 50 times, *ib.*; *constitution* (as applied to the Articles of Confederation, or as distinguished therefrom), about 27 times, *ib.*; *nation, national*, applied to both old Confederation and new Constitution, in all over 60 times, *ib.* The above summary is rather ultra conservative in its approximation of the numbers of times these several terms are found in Elliot's *Debates*.

this constitution BETWEEN THE STATES so ratifying the same." Mark you these most significant words, *between the States*. It is not provided that the ratification of this Constitution by a prescribed majority of the whole people of the then existing United States under the Articles of Confederation shall establish it over the whole people of all those United States (a provision that would have been an utter nullity, for stubborn historical reasons), but that its ratification by a certain number of the States shall establish it between – *not over*, but BETWEEN – those particular States, and none others, unless and until such others shall also ratify, each for itself.

Bearing in mind this Article VII of the Federal Constitution, the preamble becomes plain. A cardinal canon of construction is, that if possible all the parts of a written instrument shall be so construed as to be harmonious with each other. The "people of the United States," then, here means the people (or, peoples) of those several distinct States which may elect to establish the proposed Constitution *between* themselves. And indeed, this Constitution of 1787, and the Union under it, first went into effect between eleven of the States, only, as we have remarked above; North Carolina and Rhode Island remaining separate and independent republics until, after President Washington's inauguration, they chose, each for itself, to come into the new Union or confederacy.

So we see that Mr. Webster's centralist construction of the word or phrase, "the people," as used in the Constitution, falls to the ground. But again, Webster denies that the States *acceded* to the Constitution; and mark well his daring and all-important admission, that *"the natural converse of accession is secession."*

Now, it so happens that this word *accede*, or its derivative *accession*, which he thus spurns, is found, in the very sense which he denies to it, over and over again in the debates of those who framed and adopted the Constitution, and at least once in the course of the official documents pertaining to its adoption; over and over again, I say, or some forty times, by actual count, either certainly or probably in this sense, and more than twenty times unquestionably so. To give but three instances here:

James Madison said, in the Virginian convention of 1788 that debated and, by a close majority, ratified the system for Virginia: "Suppose eight States only should ratify, and Virginia should propose certain alterations as the previous condition of her *accession*."[5] In the North Carolina State convention Governor Johnston said: "We

5. Elliot's *Debates*, Vol. II., p. 165.

are not to *form* a constitution, but to say whether we [i.e., the people of North Carolina] shall *adopt* a constitution to which ten States have already *acceded*."[6] And the ratifying convention of New York (of which Alexander Hamilton was a member) prepared by unanimous order a circular letter containing this language: "Our attachment to our sister States, and the confidence we repose in them can not be more forcibly demonstrated than by *acceding* to a government which many of us think very imperfect."[7]

Webster was right; "secession is the converse of accession." Moreover, as we have seen above,[8] at least three States, Virginia, Rhode Island and New York, in their formal acts of ratification of the Federal Constitution, expressly and explicitly reserved this right of secession or peaceable withdrawal; a fact *now* well known and *now* generally acknowledged, by South and North alike.

---

6. *Ibid.*, Vol. IV., p. 183.
7. *Ib.*, p. 327.
8. *Chapter Two,* note 8.

CHAPTER FOUR

☆ ☆ ☆ ☆

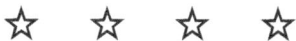

Another question asked in those debates
of the early 'thirties was, as stated above, *How
shall disputed questions of constitutional rights
and powers be decided?* By the Federal Supreme
Court, said Webster, so as to bind even sovereign
States, and in all cases. "No," said South Carolina, in substance, speaking through Hayne and
Calhoun; "the Constitution of the United States
empowers the Federal Supreme Court to decide
only 'all cases *in law and equity* arising under
this constitution, the laws of the United States,
and treaties made . . . under their authority.'"
That is the language of the Constitution: "all
cases in law and equity." And questions of sovereignty, argued South Carolina, come not within
the scope of cases in law and equity, which are
limited, by the well known common-law use of
the term, to an altogether different class of cases.

The historical correctness of this contention of
South Carolina's is supported by James Madison
in his journal of the Constitutional Constitution.
Madison, the reporter, says of himself, the delegate:

"James Madison doubted whether it was
not going too far to extend the jurisdiction of the
Federal supreme court generally to cases arising
under the constitution, and whether it ought not
to be *limited to cases of a judiciary nature.*" (The
contention of Hayne and Calhoun, exactly.)

"The right of expounding the constitution
in cases not of this nature ought not to be given
to that department.

"The [pending] motion of Dr. Johnson was
agreed to *nem. con.*, it being generally supposed
that the jurisdiction given was constructively
limited to cases of a judiciary nature."[1]

----

1. Elliot's *Debates*, Vol. V., p. 483. Just a word here as to
the man here quoted as authority, James Madison of Virginia, "father of the Constitution." From the standpoint of
a constitutional constructionist, Madison's career was
somewhat that of a pendulum. Rather centralistic at the
time of the general Constitution of 1787 that framed the
Constitution and submitted it to the States for ratification
or rejection – certainly moderately so, as disclosed by his
own utterances, from time to time, in the debates of that
Constitution, a very few years later he became Jefferson's
own right-hand man in opposing the radically centralistic

As if to clinch the matter beyond a peradventure, the words "in law and equity" were afterward inserted into the jurisdiction clause here discussed.

But if not the Federal Supreme Court, then what tribunal, inquired Webster and the North, is to decide these disputed questions of sovereignty and of constitutional powers? The answer was ready to hand: Not to the Federal Supreme Court, itself but a component part of the created central Government, where three men (a majority of a quorum of the court), and they political appointees, may have the deciding voice, must a sovereign creator State submit questions affecting her sovereign powers. She herself will decide it pending an appeal, in the true spirit of Magna Charta, to the judgment of her peers, her sister sovereign creator States in general Constitution assembled. This contention had had the support of Thomas Jefferson in 1821, as quoted by Hayne: "It is a fatal heresy to suppose that either

---

trend of the Adams administration; in his old age, and at the time of the Nullification crisis which we are now discussing, he seems to have reverted toward his earlier position. As a centralist, then, at the time he took part in and reported the debates of the general Constitutional Constitution of 1787, whatever Madison noted down of a contrary tendency is deserving of special attention and weight.

our State governments are superior to the Federal, or the Federal to the State; neither is authorized literally to decide what belongs to itself, or its co-partner in government, in differences between their different sets of public servants; the appeal is to neither, but to their employers *peaceably* assembled by their representatives in convention."[2]

More than twenty years before this utterance Jefferson had embodied this same principle in his draft of the famous Kentucky Resolutions.[3] Again, Jefferson wrote, "This *peaceable* and legitimate resource, a general convention of the States, to which we are in the habit of implicit obedience, *superseding all appeal to force*, and being always within our reach, shows a precious principle of self-preservation in our composition. . . ."[4]

Mark this: Jefferson says that in this plan of a general Constitution of the States to decide such mooted questions of constitutional construction and governmental powers, is found a *peaceable settlement* of vexing political and sectional problems. This was precisely Carolina's

---

2. "A Titans' War," chap. 15.

3. Stephens' *History of the United States*, pp. 937-39.

4. *Writings of Thomas Jefferson* (1897), Vol. VIII., pp. 22-3.

plea in 1830-33.

Right or wrong, thundered President Jackson, these Federal laws must be obeyed unless and until repealed by the same power (Congress) that enacted them, or unless and until declared unconstitutional by the Federal Supreme Court; and if not voluntarily obeyed, then obedience shall be enforced by the fratricidal sword. To like effect argued Webster. You have the right, said he, to resist laws deemed oppressive, if you so please – but it is the right of revolution, no more; justifiable only if successful, and if not successful, subject to the dread penalties of high treason.

Ours is a constitutional remedy, Hayne replied, *and a peaceable one*.[5] The right of revolution exists independently of the Constitution. That instrument expressly declares that all powers not delegated to the central Government remains to the several States, or the people; that is, to the people of those several States. This power of deciding the constitutionality or the unconstitutionality of laws of Congress, being not given in the Constitution either to Congress or to the

5. We here briefly epitomize the substance of the respective arguments of Hayne and Webster on this point. For their own language *in extenso* see the contemporaneous publication, Gales & Seaton's *Register of Debates in Congress*.

Federal Supreme Court, remains to the several States. Ours is a peaceable remedy – unless you of the North force on us the issue of war. And only if honor with peace within the Union be found no longer possible, then will we exercise that other peaceable remedy of secession or withdrawal from the partnership of States in order that, like Abraham and Lot of old, we may dwell apart in peace, rather than remain together in dissension. And if you, like George III., still pursue us with hostile intent and the sword be drawn, then upon you of the North, not upon us, must the awful responsibility rest.

For answer to this plea of peace by South Carolina, Jackson, Webster and the North passed the Force Bill, as it was called, of 1833; a bill providing for the enforcement of the tariff laws, if need be, by force of arms. But at the same time, in view of South Carolina's determined front, and signs of growing support for her from other Southern States, Jackson and Congress passed, also, the Clay Compromise bill scaling down the tariff to meet Carolina's demands.

So ended the matter for the time. The sword was threatened but not drawn, and South Carolina's *peaceable* remedy for an oppressed sectional minority prevailed. And mark this: State nullification or State veto, as here preached by Hayne and Calhoun and practiced by their native State, was a qualified nullification only, a fact too often entirely overlooked; an interposition of the State's sovereignty pending an appeal to a three-fourths decision of the confederated States in general Constitution. It was, in effect, a federal referendum.[6] It was strictly conservative of true constitutional principles. For, let us repeat, a prime object of the Federal Constitution was the *protection of the rights of the minority.*

This struggle of the early 'thirties of the nineteenth century was, as Calhoun averred at the time,[7] a contest between *power*, or the North, and *liberty*, or the South. Calhoun drew a close parallel between that contest and that other of 1776, with Northern unjust taxation of the South in 1833 bearing a marked analogy to the British unjust taxation of the American colonies in 1776.

That both of these contentions of South Carolina (i.e., qualified nullification, with secession in reserve) were sound, historically and constitutionally sound, we have just seen. That the contrary contention of Webster was unsound, unconstitutional and unhistorical, must necessarily follow. Daniel Webster has been called the "Ex-

6. See the author's article, *Federal Initiative and Referendum*, in *South Atlantic Quarterly* for October, 1912.
7. Jenkins' *Calhoun*, p. 300.

pounder of the Constitution."[8] I respectfully
submit that great "Confounder of the Constitution" would be a more fitting title. His admirer
and biographer, and a successor to him in the
Federal Senate from Massachusetts, Hon. Henry
Cabot Lodge, says of Webster's argument here:
"The weak places in his armor were historical in
their nature."[9] Of Webster on a somewhat similar
occasion the same writer says: "But the speech
is strongly partisan and exhibits the disposition
of an advocate to fit the constitution to his particular case."[10] Likewise, Webster's apologist, von
Holst, discussing this very debate with Calhoun,
sadly confesses that, "To his and his country's
harm, the advocate in him always spoke loudly
in the reasoning of the statesman."[11]

Yes, Daniel Webster was a great lawyer,
an able advocate, a magnificent orator. But as a
constitutional student he was superficial. The close
of his speech known as "Webster's reply to Hayne"
is a burst of splendid oratory, and is known and
quoted far and wide. Only less eloquent, far more

8. Brown & Strauss' *Dictionary of American Politics*, p.
153, article, "Expounder of the Constitution."

9. Lodge's *Life of Daniel Webster*, p. 171.

10. *Ibid.*, pp. 225-6.

11. Von Hoist, *Constitutional and Political History of
the United States*, Vol. I., p. 496.

sound, is the little known peroration to Hayne's rejoinder, which should be called "Hayne's reply to Webster." Mr. Webster said:

"While the union lasts we have high, exciting, gratifying prospects spread out before us, for us and our children. Beyond that I seek not to penetrate the veil. God grant that, in my day at least, that curtain may not rise. God grant that on my vision never may be opened what lies behind. When my eyes shall be turned to behold for the last time the sun in heaven, may I not see him shining on the broken and dishonored fragments of a once glorious Union; on States dissevered, discordant, belligerent; on a land rent with civil feud, or drenched, it may be, in fraternal blood! Let their last feeble and lingering glance rather behold the gorgeous ensign of the republic, now known and honored throughout the earth, still full high advanced, its arms and trophies streaming in their original lustre, not a stripe erased or polluted, not a single star obscured – bearing for its motto no such miserable interrogatory as, *What is all this worth?* nor those other words of delusion and folly, *Liberty first, and union afterwards;* but everywhere, spread all over in characters of living light, blazing on all its ample folds, as they float over the sea and over the land, and in every wind under the whole heavens, that other sentiment, dear to every true American heart –

Liberty *and* Union, now and forever, one and inseparable!"[12]

Grand, glorious – rhetorically; but it is not logic – nor yet history. According to Webster, the perpetuity of the then existing American Union was essential to the continued enjoyment of liberty. But the Declaration of Independence, mindful of the rise and fall of nations and the ever recurring changes in governments, tells us that all governments are but means to an end, and that end the securing of life, liberty and the pursuit of happiness; that here, as in any other case, when a particular means fails to effect the end in view, it should be discarded for some other means. Forgetful, too, was Webster of Washington's language in his revered Farewell Address, wherein he denominates the Union under the Constitution of 1787-9 an "experiment," and warns against "geographical discriminations" as "causes which may disturb our union." To like effect to this last, as seen above, spoke Jefferson on "the Missouri question"; but these solemn admonitions, of Washington and of Jefferson, Webster and, after him, Lincoln, heeded not.

Thus Mr. Webster in 1833, for union at any cost, when those whom he opposed themselves

---

12. See, *inter al.*, *The Speeches of Daniel Webster* (Tefft), 438.

opposed the tariff laws which, by means of "geo-graphical discriminations," favored his own New England and the North. To far different effect had he spoken some seventeen years before when, a member of the House of Representatives from New Hampshire, he voiced New England's fierce opposition to the then raging war with old England and to the pending enlistment bill for carrying on that war: "I use not the tone of intimidation or menace," thundered young Representative Webster, "but I forewarn you of consequences. . . . I beseech you, by the best hopes of your country's prosperity – by your regard for the *preservation of her government and her union* – that you abandon your system of restrictions – that you abandon it at once and abandon it forever."[13]

But to return to the Great Debate of 1830. Said Gen. Hayne in reply to Webster's "reply":

"The gentleman has made an eloquent appeal to our hearts in favor of union. Sir, I cordially respond to that appeal. I will yield to no gentleman here in sincere attachment to the union; but it is a union founded on the Constitution, and not such a union as that gentleman would give us, that is dear to my heart. If this is to become one great 'consolidated government,' swallowing up the rights of the States, and the liber-

13. *Annals of Congress, 1813-14*, Vol. I., pp. 949-50.

ties of the citizen, 'riding over the plundered ploughmen and beggared yeomanry,' the union will not be worth preserving. Sir, it is because South Carolina loves the union, and would preserve it forever, that she is opposing now, while there is hope, those usurpations of the Federal Government which, once established, will, sooner or later, tear this union into fragments.

"The gentleman is for marching under a banner, studded all over with stars, and bearing the inscription, Liberty and Union. I had thought, sir, the gentleman would have borne a standard, displaying in its ample folds a brilliant sun, extending its golden rays from the center to the extremities, in the brightness of whose beams the 'little stars hide their diminished heads.' Ours, sir, is the banner of the constitution; the twenty-four stars are there, in all their undiminished lustre; on it is inscribed, Liberty – the Constitution – Union. We offer up our fervent prayers to the Father of all Mercies that it may continue to wave, for ages yet to come, over a free, a happy, and a united people."[14]

Hayne has been criticised as having violated a cardinal rule of oratory and having attempted

---

14. "A Titans' War," chap. 15; Vol. 6, Gale & Seaton's *Register of Debates in Congress*, Part 1, abt. p. 92.

to equal Webster's peroration in his own.[15] But another view may be urged. The ablest generals – such as Lee, Jackson and Napoleon – are often those who, on occasions, transgress fundamental canons of strategy; success as a result being their only justification. Hayne, at once orator, patriot and logician, both felt the power of Webster's closing plea and its glowing imagery as it would appeal to men, and perceived its basic fallacy as applied. He proceeded, boldly and deliberately, to borrow his great antagonist's own figure of speech and turn it against him. In the brief space of the closing four sentences of the peroration just quoted, Hayne reproduces in outline the picture drawn so fully and so masterfully by Webster, dissects it, suggests a more fitting one to accord with his opponent's expressed principles, appropriates the original as properly illustrating his own position, and ends with the "fervent" and pertinent invocation that it may long be suffered to remain the true emblem of a people *free* and *happy* as well as united.

Hayne's peroration is not so elaborate or ornate as Webster's; nor was it meant to be. But it is perfect in itself. The keen, logical criticism, blended with the quiet, delicate sarcasm conveyed

---

15. Theo. D. Jervey's *Robert Y. Hayne and His Times*, p. 260.

in the reference to the "brilliant sun" and the "little stars," is exquisite; the true application of Webster's stellar picture is simple and effective. After the "fire, the wind, and the earthquake" of Webster's mighty finish it comes – as a still small voice.

And so the South triumphed with and through this remedy of peaceable protection for a sectional minority. The North, thus baffled, next resorted to a wily flank move.

CHAPTER FIVE

☆　☆　☆　☆

The next great sectional crisis (after the preliminary and premonitory one of 1850) came nearly a third of a century later. In the crisis just discussed, involving the Nullification clash of 1830-33, the tariff was the bone of contention. In this second crisis, Negro slavery in the territories was the occasion, not the cause as is imagined by many who should know better.

What was the actual source of this "free-soil" or "anti-slavery" crusade of the North? An aroused moral sense, say some. Fanaticism, say others. Partly each of these, but not exclusively or chiefly either or both, say I.

Mark well this fact: In the debates in Congress on the tariff dispute of 1833, John Quincy Adams, ex-President of the United States and then a member of the House of Representatives, uttered this significant remark from the floor of the House: "But protection might be extended in different forms to different interests. . . . In the Southern and Southwestern portion of the union, there exists a certain interest [by which Adams meant Negro slavery] which enjoys under the constitution and the laws of the United States an especial protection, peculiar to itself"[1] (i.e., return of fugitive slaves escaping from one State into another). He referred to the slaves in the Southern States as "machinery," and added, "If they [the Southern States] must withdraw protection from the free White labor of the North [the "protection" of a high tariff, Adams meant], then it ought to be withdrawn from the machinery of the South."

Ah – here we have the milk in the cocoanut; or perhaps it would be appropriate to say, the African in the fuel heap. In the framing of the Federal Constitution, the North and the South – rather, New England and the far Southern States – arranged a *quid pro quo*,[2] by which the shipping interests of New England obtained control, and permanent control, of commercial regulations by a mere majority vote, instead of a two-thirds vote, in the Congress, and the South

1. *Register of Debates in Congress*, Vol. IX., p. 1612 *et seq.*

2. Elliot's *Debates*, Vol. IV., p. 285.

(together with the slave-importing shippers of this same New England) defeated the possibility of prohibition of the continued importation of Negroes, temporarily, or for some nineteen years. And now, her darling of sectional customs "protection" in danger from South Carolina's firm stand, New England, through John Quincy Adams as her spokesman, gave warning, in 1833, that tariff "protection," although not guaranteed by the Constitution, and slavery protection, which was expressly guaranteed by that instrument, must be held as twin special interests, to stand or fall together.

In this light, then, these remarks of Adams, of Massachusetts, should be carefully marked and constantly borne in mind in connection with the subsequent growth and course of anti-Southern agitation, under the guise of an anti-slavery crusade, from the time – this time of South Carolina's Nullification stand and the resultant tariff reduction of 1833 – that a definite check was placed upon high tariff, North-favoring legislation. And this is the same Mr. Adams who shortly thereafter began to make his declining years renowned by pouring into the House of Representatives at Washington his broadsides of "anti-slavery" or anti-Southern petitions.

Finally, a new party was formed, with its primary object, as professed, the exclusion of the

South with her constitutionally-guaranteed property from the common territories that had been acquired by the common blood and the common treasure of the South and the North. And, significantly, early in its history, or as soon (1860) as it had acquired material growth and substantial prestige, this new political party, already thus avowedly sectional in its principles, made a sectional "protective" tariff one of its demands.[3] And when it had elected a President (by a sectional and a minority popular vote, be it remembered) and so caused a disruption of the Union of States, "protection" was a primary means employed to support the war that followed – a war of aggression and conquest waged by this party to secure both its own continued supremacy and the new consolidated and un-American union of force in place of the pristine confederated Union of choice which itself had done so much to destroy; a war in which Negro emancipation *in parts of the Southern States* was incidentally proclaimed *as a military measure*, the Thirteenth Amendment coming later to extend and validate this unconstitutional proceeding.

"Un-American union of force," I said; we must remember widespread opposition to the war

3. Brown & Strauss' *Dictionary of American Politics*, p. 344, article, "Republican Party."

of conquest against the South manifested itself in the North, and that the myriads of immigrants from centralist, "blood-and-iron" Germany had much to do with turning the scale in the North in support of Lincoln's and Seward's war.[4] In these aliens there had arisen "a new king which knew not Joseph," who had no inconvenient recollections of '76 to hold him in check.[5]

This so-called free-soil movement were more accurately styled a White-soil movement. For hand in hand with the efforts to keep Negro slaves out of the new States and territories of the North and the West, went drastic anti-free-Negro laws in those regions as well as in the older Nor-

---

4. See the article, "The War Day by Day," the *Washington Herald*, March 13, 1914, where we are told that the appointment of the German, Gen. Franz Sigel, early in 1864, to command in western Virginia and the Shenandoah Valley had been made by Lincoln "in pursuance of his earnest wish to recognize in every way possible the great aid Gen. Sigel's countrymen were giving the Government in the prosecution of the war. Lincoln, in homely phrase, had said that he ought to 'take care of the Germans.' Gen. Sigel's appointment was directly due to this purpose of the President's. An election was approaching and the German vote was important."

5. The foregoing was originally written *before* the outbreak of the European war of 1914, much of the responsibility for which must be laid to the charge of this same "blood-and-iron" nation.

thern States.[6] The Negro, slave or free, was not wanted in the North and West. Long since had Jefferson, the honest abolitionist, pointed out that, "The passage of slaves from one State to another would not make a slave of a single human being who would not be so without it. So their diffusion over a greater surface would make them individually happier and proportionally facilitate the accomplishment of their emancipation by dividing the burden on a greater number of coadjutors."[7] This warning, like those other warnings of Jefferson and Washington above mentioned, of course went unheeded by the Negro-exclusionists of the North and Northwest.

---

6. These laws are to be found discussed most illuminatingly in Ewing's *Legal and Historical Status of the Dred Scott Decision*, Chapter Four. See, also, *Northern Rebellion and Southern Secession*, by the same author, page 113.

7. As quoted in Stephens' *History of the United States*, p. 432.

CHAPTER SIX

☆　☆　☆　☆

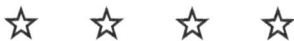

Nullification, or State veto subject to federal referendum, was practicable in 1833; practicable and successful. In 1860-61 it was not practicable, because a State could not exercise her veto power out in the common territories, where the sectional, Northern party that had just been elected to power threatened anti-Southern legislation. Hence, when peace with honor was no longer possible within the Union of States, the Southern States turned to the only possible peaceable alternative, secession, or complete withdrawal from that inter-State compact of government already so flagrantly violated, in act and in promise of further acts to come, by their Northern sisters.

That the voice and efforts, the counsels and measures of the Southland were still for peace, the record abundantly proves.

Sturdy little South Carolina, faithful to the spirit of her departed Hayne and Calhoun, was the first State to withdraw. On her invitation, delegates from five other of the "cotton States" that followed her in withdrawing, and later those from a sixth, Texas, met her own delegates in a Congress at Montgomery, Alabama, February 4, 1861. By this Congress was framed the provisional Constitution of the Confederate States of America. Jefferson Davis, of Mississippi, was chosen provisional President of the new union.

On February 15, 1861, before the arrival of Mr. Davis at Montgomery to take the oath of office, the Congress passed a resolution providing, "that a commission of three persons be appointed by the President-elect as early as may be convenient after his inauguration, and sent to the Government of the United States, for the purpose of negotiating *friendly* relations between that Government and the Confederate States of America, and for the settlement of all questions of disagreement between the two governments, upon principles of right, justice, equity and good faith."[1]

Truly, as Mr. Stephens, of Georgia, one of the delegates to this Montgomery Congress, says

---

1. Stephens, *History of the United States*, p. 602; *Messages and Papers of the Confederacy*, Vol. I., p. 55.

in his history of the United States, these "were not such men as revolutions or civil commotions usually bring to the surface. . . . Their object was not to tear down, so much as it was to build up with the greater security and permanency."[2] And we may add that they meant to build up, if so permitted, peaceably.

In this spirit of amity and justice, the first act of the Louisiana State convention, after passing the ordinance of secession, was to adopt, unanimously, a resolution recognizing the right to free navigation of the Mississippi river (which flows down from the Northern States of the great inland basin and empties into the sea within the confines of Louisiana), and further recognizing the right of egress and ingress at that river's mouth and looking to the guaranteeing of these rights.[3]

President Davis' inaugural address, delivered February 18, 1861, breathed the same spirit of friendship toward our brothers of the North. He said, in part:

"Our present political position has been achieved in a manner unprecedented in the history of nations. It illustrates *the American idea that governments rest on the consent of the gov-*

---

2. *Ibid.*, p. 598.

3. Official Journal Louisiana Convention of 1861, No. 3 of the ordinances and resolutions passed.

erned, and that it is the right of the people to alter or abolish them at will whenever they become destructive of the ends for which they were established. The declared purpose of the compact of the union from which we have withdrawn was to 'establish justice, *insure domestic tranquility,*[4] provide for the common defense, promote the general welfare, and secure the blessings of liberty to ourselves and our posterity;' and when, in the judgment of the sovereign States composing this Confederation, it has been perverted from the purposes for which it was ordained, and ceased to answer the ends for which it was established, a *peaceful appeal* to the ballot box declared that, so far as they are concerned, the Government created by that compact should cease to exist. In this they merely asserted the right which the Declaration of Independence of July 4, 1776, defined to be 'inalienable.' . . .

"Thus the sovereign States here represented have proceeded to form this Confederacy; and it is by abuse of language that their act has been denominated a revolution. They formed a new alliance, but within each State its government has remained; so that the rights of person and property have not been disturbed. The agent

---

4. Here and elsewhere, in quotations found in this article, the emphasis is our own.

through which they communicated with foreign nations is changed, but this does not necessarily interrupt their international relations. Sustained by the consciousness that the transition from the former union to the present Confederacy has not proceeded from a disregard on our part of just obligations, or any failure to perform every constitutional duty, moved by no interest or passion to invade the rights of others, *anxious to cultivate peace* and commerce with all nations, if we may not hope to avoid war, we may at least expect that posterity will acquit us of having needlessly engaged in it. . . .

"An agricultural people, whose chief interest is the export of commodities required in every manufacturing country, *our true policy is peace,* and the freest trade which our necessities will permit. . . . If a just perception of mutual interest shall permit us *peaceably* to pursue our separate political career, my most earnest desire will have been fulfilled. But if this be denied to us, and the integrity of our territory and jurisdiction be assailed, it will but remain for us with firm resolve to appeal to arms and invoke the blessing of Providence on a just cause."[5]

Nor did our President content himself with

---

5. *Messages and Papers of the Confederacy*, Vol. I., pp. 32-4.

mere *words* of peace. He promptly acted on the resolution of Congress above cited, and appointed three commissioners from our Government to the Government of the United States. "These commissioners," says Mr. Stephens, "were clothed with plenary powers to open negotiations for the settlement of all matters of joint property, forts, arsenals, arms or property of any other kind within the limits of the Confederate States, and all joint liabilities with their former associates, upon principles of right, justice, equity and good faith."[6]

Let me ask, Could anything have been fairer?

These commissioners promptly proceeded on their way. A few days after the inauguration of Mr. Lincoln at Washington they formally notified his Secretary of State, Mr. Seward, that "the President, Congress and people of the Confederate States *earnestly desire a peaceful solution*" of pending questions between the two governments. The full history of these negotiations makes mighty interesting reading. But it is too long a story to be rehearsed in detail here.[7] Suf-

---

6. Stephens' *History of the United States,* p. 604.

7. *Ibid.,* pp. 607-9 and Appendix N; also, *Messages and Papers of the Confederacy*, Vol. I., pp. 63 *et seq.* and pp. 82 *et. seq.* (Messages of President Davis to Congress, April 29, 1861, and May 8, 1861.)

fice it to say that it was through no fault of these commissioners, or of the people and government they represented, that their mission of peace and good will to their late allies of the North came to naught.

South Carolina, shortly after her secession in December, 1860, had taken like steps looking to peace, by sending a commission to negotiate with Buchanan's administration relative to former United States property within her limits.[8]

Yet another effort for peace was made from a Southern official quarter in those portentous, ominous months following the sectional victory at the polls in November, 1860. The provisional Confederate Constitution mentioned above was framed and adopted by what were called the seven Cotton States. The border Southern States were yet within the old Union, hoping against hope for continued union, peace and justice. Among these border States was Virginia, the oldest, the most powerful of them all. By unanimous vote of her Legislature all the States of the Union were invited to send commissioners to a conference, to devise some plan for preserving harmony and constitutional union.[9]

This conference met in Washington, Febru-

8. Stephens' *History of the United States*, p. 604.

9. *Ibid.*, p. 589; E. A. Pollard's *The Lost Cause*, p. 94.

ary 4, 1861, the very day on which the Congress of the seceded Cotton States assembled in Montgomery. It adjourned February 27. Significantly enough, in view of our present argument, this conference at Washington was called the *Peace Congress*. The demands or suggestions of the South in this Peace Congress were only that constitutional obligations should be observed by all parties; nay, that certain concessions to the North would be agreed to, by means of constitutional amendment, if only the Constitution, as thus amended, might be obeyed. This did not suit the commissioners from the Northern States, as was bluntly stated by one of them, then and there – Salmon P. Chase, of Ohio, who was slated for a portfolio in Lincoln's cabinet, and therefore spoke at least *quasi et cathedra*. So the Peace Congress proved of no avail.[10]

We find a similar situation in the Congress of the United States at its regular session that winter. Of the condition there Mr. Pollard says, in his book, *The Lost Cause*: "It is remarkable that of all the compromises proposed in this Congress for preserving the peace of the country, none came from Northern men; they came from

10. See this more fully discussed in Stephens' *History of the United States*, pp. 590 et seq.

the South and were defeated by the North."[11]

Well might the Southern leaders have adopted for their own the language of the Psalmist, "I am for peace: but when I speak, they are for war."[12]

It was by virtue of this impossible condition arising within the old Union that Southern States, cotton and border, one by one, found it necessary to withdraw from that Union – which was effected so far as possible, in every instance, *peaceably*. They had not only the historical, constitutional right to do this, as every real student of constitutional history, South and North, now admit; they had, further, let us here repeat, the general assertion of the Declaration of Independence, governing all like cases, to support them. As pointed out by President Davis, in the above quotation from his inaugural, a prime object in establishing the Constitution of the United States and the federative Government thereunder, was to "insure domestic tranquility." The existing form of government under this Constitution having "become destructive of this end," so far as concerned the Southern States, the peoples of these States now moved to peaceably alter the form of government.

---

11. *The Lost Cause*, 93.
12. The Bible, Psalm cxx, 7.

And, seldom remembered though it be now, there were at that time many in the North who believed that these Southern peoples had the inalienable right thus peaceably to withdraw. For instance, the *New York Tribune* itself, organ though it was of the aggressive anti-Southern party of that time, declared in November and December, 1860, after Lincoln's election, as follows:

"We hold with Jefferson to the inalienable right of communities to alter or abolish forms of government that have become oppressive or injurious, and if the Cotton States shall become satisfied that they can do better out of the Union than in it, we insist on letting them *go in peace.* The right to secede may be a revolutionary one, but it exists nevertheless, and we do not see how one party can have a right to do what another party has the right to prevent. Whenever a considerable section of our union shall deliberately decide to go out, we shall resist all coercive measures designed to keep it in. *We hope never to live in a republic whereof one section is pinned to the residue by bayonets. . . .* If ever seven or eight States send agents to Washington to say, 'We want to go out of the union,' we shall feel constrained by our devotion to human liberty to say, 'Let them go!' And we do not see how we could take the other side, without coming in direct conflict with those rights of man which we hold paramount to all political arrangements, however convenient and advantageous."[13]

Not such men as *revolutions* generally bring to the front, said Stephens, of the Confederate leaders. True. For be it remembered that these men represented, officially represented, long existent and independent republics, already fully ` organized. The formation of a league or confederacy between these republics was but an incident, an arrangement of convenience, as pointed out by Mr. Davis in his inaugural address. How, then, could States, republics, independent nations, be said to revolt or rebel? A people or a faction rebels against a superior; *not* against an equal or an inferior. Therefore, a creator State of inherently sovereign powers could not possibly rebel against either the creature central Government of strictly limited and delegated powers, or against co-equal, confederate States. This being so, and Southern individuals acting only as citizens of their respective States, there could be no treason in their conduct.

Why was Jefferson Davis, although long held a prisoner after the war, never brought to trial on the charge of high treason for which he was indicted? It is said (though I am not at this time prepared to vouch for the accuracy of the re-

---

13. As quoted in *The Lost Cause*, pp. 84-5.

port) that a solemn warning was sounded forth from the Supreme Court of the United States to the effect that to push such a charge against our fallen leader would be to fool with a combination boomerang and back-action buzz-saw. Be that as it may, we know that Mr. Davis, after long imprisonment, was released on bail (Horace Greeley himself being a bondsman), and the indictment' was never tried.

Yes, the course of the Southern peoples was the only course consistent with *peace and honor*. Alas! they were ahead of their times; and, like all those who, in any age or clime, dare to be ahead of their day and generation, they have been made to suffer for their temerity. As Charles Mackay, the poet says:

> "That man is thought a knave or fool,
> Or bigot plotting crime,
> Who, for the advancement of his race,
> I*s wiser than his time.*"

CHAPTER SEVEN
☆ ☆ ☆ ☆

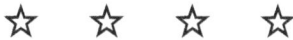

Civilization takes but one step forward at a time; then pauses and rests before the next step. The Southern people of the period of 1789-1861, in the very vanguard of this slowly advancing civilization, acted on the principle that the same rule should govern in the intercourse between nations and people as between individuals – and that rule the golden rule. But they were wiser than their time. Let me explain.

Some three centuries before this the civilized, Christian (?) nations of Europe saw nothing wrong in kidnapping the defenseless heathens of African sands and selling them into bondage far from their native haunts. They justified such practice on the grounds alike of expediency and morals. It would bring the heathen under the benign influences of Christianity, and at the same time cause wealth to flow into the ready pockets of their benignant captors. So the over-sea slave trade went merrily on for the space of several hundreds of years. Then laggard civilization took a step forward, and said that this was all wrong. The African trade, or the theft and forcible importation of Negroes was abolished, and the Southern States took a hand with the rest in abolishing it. Meantime, civilization was preparing to take another step forward to supplement the cessation of slave importation with the abolition of slavery itself. Owing to local causes some communities were more forward in this movement than were others. The situation in the Southern States was thus sensed by Jefferson:

"The cession of that kind of property [slaves], for so it is misnamed, is a bagatelle which would not cost me a second thought if in that way a general emancipation and expatriation could be effected; and gradually with due sacrifice I think it might be, but as it is we have the wolf by the ears and we can neither hold him nor safely let him go. Justice is in the one scale and self-preservation in the other."[1]

Too, it should be added, slavery remained profitable in the South longer than in some other communities, and Southerners were but human.

1. *The Writings of Thomas Jefferson* (1829), Vol. IV., p. 324.

But the reform was moving forward everywhere, and was bound to triumph in the end. *It ought to have been allowed to triumph peaceably.* Out of the differences in local conditions, in this and in other matters, arose the fierce controversies between the Southern and the Northern States of the American Union.

When the contention had waxed so hot that peaceful union was no longer possible, then the Southern States proposed a peaceable separation. The North said, No; we will force you back. The South said, No; that is all wrong. The Declaration of Independence, the letter and the spirit of the Constitution, advancing civilization itself, all proclaim in trumpet tones that it is just as wrong for one nation, State or group of States to conquer another *vi et armis* and to force upon it a government it does not desire, as it is for one man to steal another man and sell him into bondage, or for a nation now (as was formerly done) to deny to its citizens the right of voluntary expatriation.

So spoke the South, wiser than her time. The North, not so wise, essayed to enslave whole States and peoples. For this is what a forcible union of one-time sovereign States means.

It is not within the scope of this address to follow the course of that memorable struggle. From the day of Thermopylæ down, to battle for home and native land against the invader and the despoiler has ever called forth the utmost valor and exertion of patriots. The Southern soldiery came of an adventurous, frontier stock; generally could ride and shoot; and in this war they fought to repel the invader. The result was the Confederate warrior, since that time the synonym for all that is best and bravest in war. The fame of the Confederate soldier is deathless; his glory as eternal as the stars. Starvation, not numbers, overwhelmed him after four years of heroic endurance and brilliant feats of arms. The Crucial Banner of the South sank without a stain upon it, save only the lifeblood of thousands of its martyr defenders.

In this course of invasion and conquest, in which she was finally successful, did the North, let me ask, really "save the Union," as she professed to do? No, she did not – from the very nature of the thing, she could not. The Union of the fathers, of the Constitution of 1787-89, was a union of choice, of peace. That original Union was and is forever gone, as between the South and the North. It was *ipso facto* destroyed by the withdrawal from it of the Southern States. And, like Humpty Dumpty when he fell from the wall, or like the late Mr. Morgan's scrambled eggs, all the king's horses and all the king's men could never (forcibly) put it together again. *A* union, indeed, a new, diverse, blood red union of force was created and pinned together by bayonets; *the Union was not, and could not, be saved*, though it might be *restored* by the free consent, once more, of all the parties to the original Union.

And further, the success of the Southern Confederacy would not have meant the destruction of the American Union. By the victory of the revolted colonies in 1776-83, the immemorial union of English-speaking peoples was severed; *but only as to these colonies;* the rest of the English-speaking union, known as the British Empire, continues to live, and to live truly stronger and better from the lesson that was well learned when one part of that union was lost through the blunders of sectional aggression.

Not for one moment do I question the honesty and patriotism of the brave soldiers in blue who, I cheerfully admit, sincerely believed that they were fighting for the Union of the fathers – although many of them allowed themselves to be swept along into this belief. But I do say this, that they, as well as we, were victims of their own Juggernaut; that their plea for a forcible American Union was of the same essence with the plea, in 1776, for a forcible British union. It was the plea of Old World and world-old imperialism, and *a plea which will justify every war of invasion and conquest* that has ever stained history's pages.

But the objection is sometimes made that

the South's success would have meant the Latin-Americanization of the Southern States: that, the principle of peaceable secession, once established, all union between the different States would have been no more than a rope of sand, and we would speedily have degenerated into a parcel of petty, mutually jealous republics – perhaps dictatorships. *The history of our race refutes the suggestion.*

For some two thousand years the Anglo-Saxon and the Celt have wrought out, link by link, on the anvil of hard experience and dogged experimentation, the everlasting principles of self-government. The success of the Confederate States of America would have turned out another and a stronger link, would have marked another glorious step forward in the laborious progress of Liberty and Self-Government. Ours is a patient race, no less than a progressing one, and the successful termination of our second War for Independence could never have changed that bent of mind and habit of action that stand behind the following assertion in the Declaration of Independence:

"Prudence, indeed, will dictate that governments long established should not be changed for light and transient causes; and, accordingly, all experience hath shown that mankind are more disposed to suffer, while evils are sufferable, than to right themselves by abolishing the forms to which they are accustomed."

After the triumph of our first War of Secession more than three-quarters of a century passed, during which this right of secession, as now reinforced by constitutional provisions, was often asserted, before it was actually resorted to. There is no reason to think that a second successful application of this drastic remedy, and under a like strong provocation, would have cut us adrift from our previous caution and long-suffering.

Again, it is argued that there would have been constant causes for friction and even bloodshed arising between the Confederate States of America and their neighbors to the north, the United States of America. Well, would that sort of bloodshed have been any bloodier than the four years of it that was suffered in imposing the Union's yoke upon the Southern States? But, after all, are we so sure that those two powers, once they had started together in the pathway of peace, would have been unable to continue side by side in amity? Despite strong provocation at times we manage, nearly all of the time, to preserve the peace even with storm-rocked Mexico. And we are about to celebrate a century of peace with those ancient enemies of ours, now our British and Canadian friends, although during the whole of that period they have formed our entire northern land boundary, and although "another Mississippi" (the Great Lakes and the St. Lawrence) flows from our territory through theirs to the sea.

Another objection, or theory: That, after all, it is better for the South that the War should have ended as it did. No, a thousand times no: first and foremost, because evil should never be done that good may come of it, and because Appomattox put back a half-century or more the hand of progress on the dial plate of civilization; second and secondarily, because the history of the fifty years succeeding the War is a record of legislation hostile to the material interests of the Southern portion of what is called a reunited country. Under the first of these two heads we may add, that not only was progress thus retarded, but that a new and dangerous element has been introduced into the body politic – the spirit of evasion of the fundamental law. If you doubt it, see how certain provisions of the Fourteenth Amendment to the Federal Constitution have become practically a dead letter, and by well-nigh universal consent. This Fourteenth Amendment is one of the "War amendments," as they are called.

CHAPTER EIGHT

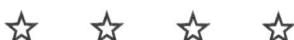

☆　☆　☆　☆

Fate, we hear it said, had decreed the downfall of the Southern Confederacy. The very stars in their courses, we are told, fought against the South, even as they fought against Sisera of yore. That assertion I shall not here stop to dispute, beyond remarking that the final outcome of the War was extremely doubtful until within less than eight months of Gen. Lee's surrender – probably so, that is, until Atlanta fell a few weeks before the date of the Presidential election of 1864 in the United States.

But – what is meant by "the stars in their courses"?

Come with me, on a clear, moonless night, and scan that part of the heavens that encircles the Pole star and in which the entire course of a given star is above the horizon. Watch with me some bright stellar sun which, having left the zenith, gradually descends the western sky, appears to stand still awhile at the extreme westernmost point, then swings slowly but surely eastward again on the return sweep around the pole, yet still descending until it reaches the nadir, whence it gradually ascends again as it swings ever on toward the east. Other stars, farther south, not thus visible throughout their entire orbits, appear to the eye of the observer to set, and are blotted out of sight a long while before they rise again.

Yes, the stars indeed march resistlessly on, in their courses; but *those courses are in circles.*

There are signs in the political heavens, that Dixie's guiding star, her glorious constellation the Southern Cross of battle, which set blood red at Appomattox, is now appearing in the east, a pure, glistening white, the day-star of hope and happiness, for the Southland and for the world.

To explain, and to drop the figure. Certain great world tendencies, in the forward march of civilized mankind, are found in diverse yet complementary pairs; first one, then the other, predominating in alternate, pulsating cycles. Broadly speaking, the nineteenth century was an era of the predominance of the centripetal power in government, the ascendancy of the central political authority. The triumph of militant French democracy in the revolution of 1789 quickly merged into the imperial despotism of Napoleon, the erstwhile republican conqueror; this was succeeded by the return of the Bourbons to power. Just at this time our Latin neighbors to the south, not yet schooled for true liberty, broke away from enervated Spain; but we must remember that it was only the joining of hands of the United States and Britain, and the resultant raising of that shield of the Western World, the Monroe Doctrine, that checked the reactionist "Holy Alliance" of continental Europe in its project of forcible recovery of these revolted Spanish colonies – so, at least, it is supposed. The Second French Republic, born out of due time in the abortive convulsions of 1848, was speedily swallowed up by the Second Empire, which eventually gave place to the Third (and semi-monarchical) Republic. The great revolutionary upheavals of 1848 throughout Europe were generally suppressed. Within the next few years Kossuth and the cause of Hungarian independence went down before the imperial Hapsburgs; Poland in vain sought to regain her lost nationality; the former independent or autonomous principalities and electorates of Germany became welded into the modern German Empire with the ruthless Bismarck at the helm.

In the face of this ominous reaction in the Old World, the glorious ensign of confederated Southern independence was raised aloft in our own stormy sky. The dragon teeth of overweening, un-

American imperialism sown by Webster thirty years before, bore their rich harvest of armed cohorts from the North, and the Southern Confederacy, latest and most promising of Freedom's growing family of happy nations, was swept from the face of the earth. And, significantly enough, in the midst of our struggle for independence, it was the fleet of autocratic Russia, inveterate foe to liberty, that wintered in New York harbor to lend moral support to the cause of Northern aggression and conquest, as against the threatened aid of more enlightened England to the cause of the South[1] – England, always the well-wisher of a weaker people fighting for freedom, except only when she herself happens to be the oppressor – England, who at a later time crushed down the liberty-loving Boers in a war in many particulars most strikingly like the war on the Confederacy.

But now, thank God, the trend amongst progressive and, at heart, liberty-loving peoples is, once more, away from imperialism and forcible union. For, under imperialism and forcible union, there is no adequate protection for a *sectional minority;* remember that. Imperialism and forcible union are, in their workings, robbery of the right

---

1. See, *inter alia*, "A Russian Alliance," editorial in *Harper's*.

of local self-government which is the alpha and omega of political liberty. From about the close of the nineteenth century on, what do we see? The waning of the centripetal force in government, the waxing of the centrifugal. In the world-old strife between Liberty and Power, Liberty begins again to prevail, in the renewed recognition of the saving principle of Home Rule and the rights of the minority.

We ourselves in 1898 helped Cuba in her stand for freedom. Five years later we aided and abetted Panama in her secession from the United States – of Colombia. We thereby officially and governmentally recognized (whether with due regard to our duty toward Colombia, we need not here inquire), solemnly recognized, that the interests and desires of the whole are not always paramount to the rights of a part; yea, even though the territorial integrity of the United States – of Colombia was thereby sacrificed. Shortly thereafter we see Norway resolutely sunder the bonds of union with her homogeneous sister, Sweden. And the wayward, weaker sister (with about the same proportion of area and population of the whole Scandinavian union as the South had of the whole American Union) is in this instance allowed to go in peace, just as certain in the North were fair enough and brave enough to advocate, but vainly, be done with us in 1861. And later still we see something like secession from secession, in the case of Ulster and Ireland.

Even in the matter of amending the Federal Constitution, behold Senator LaFollette's "gateway amendment," by which a minority is empowered to propose amendments. A similar provision was made fifty years before in the Constitution of the Confederate States of America;[2] a most decided improvement, in favor of the rights of the minority, over the cumbersome and reactionary provision of the Federal Constitution requiring a two-thirds majority even to propose amendment for consideration by the amending power.

These, I submit, are no fanciful comparisons, no imaginary parallels. No matter what may be all the details, all the motives, in each case, on the whole we may confidently affirm that through it all runs a larger sense than before of the rights of the weaker; of the beauties and blessings of peace; of the folly, and worse, of war. The Hague tribunal and the Bryan peace treaties are further witnesses to this auspicious change. To come nearer home: an acquaintance of mine, a gentleman from California, remarked casually, in the course of a conversation with me, that among the

---

2. Permanent Constitution of the Confederate States of America.

people of the Pacific coast there was quite a good deal of talk to the effect that they have their own interests and are quite capable of maintaining a separate political existence; although, he added, there is among them, too, a strong attachment to the Union. Just how these two things are reconciled, or to be reconciled he did not say. And (another coincidence) much of the differences, if such we may style them, between the Pacific States and the East, like the former controversies between South and North, arise from a race question growing out of the presence in their midst of an alien, dark-skinned race.

So we see the tardily turning tide of national and international ideals and tendencies at last following the once overwhelmed, never really lost, current of Confederate principles. And the South, the ever faithful South, of later times we find revering her leaders of the earlier and darker periods, for "there is life in the old land yet."

We find the South, near half a century after Appomattox, risen phœnix-like from the ashes of War and Reconstruction and pushing forward in all fields of endeavor. Agriculture, commerce, manufactures, education, literature, good roads, adjustment of her race problem without undue outside interference (hence, as more of a sociological, less of a partisan, sectional question) – in all these the peoples of the Southern States were making splendid progress and were rapidly recovering the lost ground in political leadership. But, in the midst of all this it was that, by separate but similar acts, three Southern States, for themselves and for the South at large, linked the present with the past for the future in a way most significant.

In the first decade of the twentieth century the South placed among the officially designated immortals of the several United States in Statuary Hall at the Capitol building in Washington city the effigies of John C. Calhoun of South Carolina, and Robert E. Lee of Virginia, and on the sterling plate service of the battleship *Mississippi* the likeness of Jefferson Davis of Mississippi and Kentucky. There they remained, fitly typifying the South's own contribution to the cause of true Liberty as against over-weening Power, her chosen champions of the two phases of constitutional home rule through State sovereignty, viz: Nullification or State veto subject to federal referendum, and Secession or resumption of full powers by the State; and only when these are scorned by her oppressors and all constitutional redress denied, then the stainless sword of defensive war.[3]

---

3. "Trusting in Almighty God, an approving conscience and the aid of my fellow-citizens, I devote myself to the service of my native State, in whose behalf alone will I

Calhoun, Davis, Lee – men with private lives as spotless as their political principles are true, exemplars of the Southland's past, guides for her future.

Yes, our constellation was only obscured, it did not really set at Appomattox; the Southern Cross of Minority Rights, Home Rule and Arbitration once more flames in the morning sky, and it shall shine more and more unto the perfect day, if the South – America – the world, is to have *true progress with Peace.*

---

ever again draw my sword." – Gen. Robert E. Lee to the Convention of Virginia, April, 1861, in accepting the command of the military forces of the State to defend her against the impending invasion: Rev. J. Wm. Jones' *Life and Letters of Robert Edward Lee* (1906), p. 135.

ADDENDUM

☆　☆　☆　☆

A few months after the original preparation and delivery of the above address, the Confederate monument at Arlington was unveiled, June 4, 1914. (Why was this not done one day earlier, President Davis' birthday?) This monument – a memorial both to the heroic Confederate dead and to the equally heroic women of the South who raised it – is a masterpiece of the great sculptor, Ezekiel, himself one of our boy heroes of the cadet corps at New Market. The female figure surmounting the pedestal and personifying the Southland holds in one hand the laurel wreath for her marytr dead – some of whom, below her, are pictured as when in life and rallying to her defense. In the other hand she holds a pruning hook, and beside her stands a plow ready for the furrow; the whole fitly typifying the genius of the

Confederacy – Peace, so far as possible,[1] and Progress.

President Wilson accepted the monument on behalf of the Federal Government. Secretary Bryan was an honored guest on the platform – two apostles of amity and justice among the nations of the earth. By this monument the Confederate States of America speak their message of peace to these our rulers, and through them to the world.

"By their fruits ye shall know them"[2] – the Southern Confederacy, like murdered Abel of old, through its "more excellent sacrifice . . . being dead yet speaketh."[3]

---

1. The Bible, Romans xii, 18.

2. *Ibid.*, Matthew vii, 20.

3. *Ibid.*, Hebrews xi, 4.

APPENDIX ONE

☆　☆　☆　☆

Davis, Lincoln, and the Kaiser

Following are some extracts from "Abraham Lincoln and the Issues of the World War," an article in the *Saturday Evening Post* of May 5, 1917, written by Mr. George Wharton Pepper, a prominent lawyer of the North (reproduced here in numbered paragraphs for convenience; italics adjusted for the purposes of the present article

1. "In the Gettysburg speech Lincoln expressed our idea of popular government in words that may become immortal. Every school child can now speak glibly about 'government of the people, by the people, and for the people.' Possibly the words are so familiar that we forget to consider their meaning." In a free, popular government the people "have grown into an *association* for the establishment of justice, for the securing of common rights, and for the promotion of

general welfare. * * * All powers not granted [to the people's "servants," "the legislators and the executive"] belong to the people."

2. "Lincoln regarded the Civil War as a test. It was, in his opinion, to determine not merely whether this nation, but whether any nation similarly conceived, could long endure. The contending parties, indeed, were both true Americans." This "was because the real issue in the Civil War was whether a government of *associated individuals* is strong enough to hold together in an internal crisis. If a popular government formed under such favorable conditions as these could not survive an acute internal difference of opinion between two *groups of citizens,* then democracy as a permanent form of government was doomed. Lincoln was right. The very conception of government by the people was on trial."

"At the bottom of the long-standing trouble between Austria and Serbia were the Austrian determination to force the imperial idea of government upon Serbia and the Serbian determination to resist it. No God-fearing man will justify the murder of the Austrian archduke. Neither will he approve the terrible international crime which Austria thereupon committed, pleading the assassination as an excuse. Austria's famous ultimatum to Serbia bore all the earmarks of a sham proposal. * * * Serbia's reply was pacific in the extreme. All the demands were conceded except the impossible two, and even as to these there was a qualified acceptance, coupled with an offer to refer the matter either to the Hague Tribunal or to the Great Powers. * * * No fair-minded man can read the diplomatic record without concluding that the Kaiser's government deliberately and successfully blocked England's earnest effort at conciliation and did so in order that the Austrian Emperor might impose on Serbia *the shackles of government from the top.*"

4. "An Awful Responsibility" – After certain conciliatory steps by both Austria and Russia, "peace prospects for a moment seemed bright. But the German Kaiser addressed to Russia a peremptory demand to stop the mobilization at once, though only by means of it had Austria been induced to pause in her insane course. The Czar's reply was conciliatory: the Kaiser's rejoinder was fiery and insolent. Russia failing to halt at the point of the pistol, Germany immediately declared war, first on Russia and then on Russia's ally, France. * * * The triumph of Russia and her allies in the war will be a notable triumph for government by the people. * * * If the State is conceived of as the foundation of rights and its interests are regarded as paramount to those of the subject, it is only a short step to the conclusion that the State is not bound by the moral principles which are

binding upon individuals. If there were a definite moral code for nations, the coexistence of two standards of conduct would be at least perplexing. But as *there is, in fact, only one standard* in the world, the refusal of a government to conform to that one standard makes of the nation an outlaw."

5. "The point to which such a State will go in violating moral principles may depend entirely upon what the ruler regards as the State's self-interest. What that self-interest is conceived at any time to be depends in turn upon the prevailing view of national destiny. * * * We know to-day what infinite suffering has resulted from the Kaiser's violation of Belgian neutrality. We realize how utterly impossible it will always be for Germany to make adequate amends for unspeakable loss. As one tragic event has succeeded another – rape following robbery and murder giving place to the torture of slavery – the words of the German Chancellor have burned themselves deeper and deeper into the consciousness of the rest of the world. 'We are now in a state of necessity,' said he; and he might have added: 'And our necessitous condition is the direct result of our own wrong.' What he actually proclaimed to the Reichstag was far different. 'Necessity,' he whined, 'knows no law.'

6. "International law would have been vio-

lated by the invasion of neutral Belgium even if there had been no express guaranty by treaty that Germany would respect that neutrality. But there was such a treaty; so that the invasion violated also the obligation of a most solemn contract. * * * There was, therefore, no possible excuse for what was done except the self-interest of the German State."

7. "The issue must not be obscured by insisting that in the course of the war cruelties have been practiced by other nations as well. It is inevitable that this should be so. But the things that individuals or nations do under provocation and in violation of their own standards are not to be compared with the outworkings of an immoral system in which these things have an avowed and legitimate place. Such is the issue between government from the top and government by the people." The people of Germany "have been trained in the most insidious ways to think of themselves more highly than they ought to think and to conceive of national self-interest as of more concern than the moral law."

In the great world war "America is privileged to spend her blood and her might for the principles which gave her birth and happiness and the peace she has treasured. God helping her, she can do no other."

Mr. Pepper's argument is, in brief, first,

that in the war of 1861 the very conception of government by the people was on trial and would have gone to everlasting smash if the Confederacy had succeeded in maintaining its independence, and this notwithstanding that both of the contending parties "were true Americans" (how this could be is not so clear); second, that nations, more particularly as concerns the great war of 1914, are bound by the same moral code which governs individuals.

It seems unfortunate at this time of common endeavor by South and North in the war with Germany that such an article should be written virtually identifying Lincoln's Government of 1861 with the allies of 1914 as the army of liberty and by the same token equally identifying the Confederate States with Germany and her allies as the foes of that liberty. But such an article *has* been written and published widely. So let us now proceed critically to examine the thesis it embodies. Let us paraphrase the above extracts so as to apply throughout to the facts and conditions of the war of 1861 and see how the logical application of Mr. Pepper's second contention affects the soundness of his first.

1. Every school child, adopting Lincoln's Gettysburg speech, can now speak glibly of "government of the people, by the people, and for the people." But the true meaning of this phrase is

not so easily grasped and retained, especially as applied to a "confederated republic," as Washington termed the United States under the Constitution of 1789.[1] These several States – i.e., the people or peoples constituting them – after separate origins and long-continued careers as separate colonies and commonwealths, grew into an association, confederation, or league in order, as expressed in the preamble, "to form a more perfect union, establish justice, insure domestic tranquillity, provide for the common defense, promote the general welfare, and secure the blessings of liberty" to the people of that generation and to their "posterity."

All powers not granted to the newly formed central Government, the creation, agent, and servant of these several States or peoples, necessarily belonged to these several free, creating States; were, moreover, expressly reserved by the Tenth Amendment to the Federal Constitution "to the States respectively, or to the people" – i.e., to the States respectively or to the people *thereof,* as must needs be from the historical nature of the case and as appears from the pertinent documents and debates of those times and as is declared by the Supreme Court of the United States in the case

1. As quoted in A. H. Stephens' *History of the United States*, p. 391.

of *Murphy vs. Ramsey* (114 United States Reports, 44).

2. The crisis of 1861 was a test. It was to determine whether institutional liberty was to be allowed *peaceably* to proceed in the way pointed out in the Declaration of Independence, where it is declared that governments derive "their just powers from the consent of the governed" and that whenever any form of government becomes destructive of its true end of securing the rights of life, liberty, and the pursuit of happiness, "it is the right of the people to alter or to abolish it and to institute a new government" – to proceed under these sublime principles of the Declaration of Independence, as supplemented by the written, contractual guaranties of the Constitution of 1789, or whether the North would follow the example of George III. and by force of arms attempt to deny these "unalienable rights" to the peoples of the Southern States.

Stated in somewhat different words, the real issue of the war of 1861 was whether a government of associated States was strong enough in self-control on the part of a sectionalist majority, then for the moment in power, to abide by the principles of 1776 and by the written conditions and guaranties of the constitutional compact and to let the aggrieved minority of the States separate in peace, like Abraham from Lot of old, when they could no longer dwell together in amity. If so, a great step forward, proclaimed in 1776 and reaffirmed in 1789, would be vindicated; if not, we would be back on pre-Revolutionary ground, when only bloody revolution was looked to as the means of redress for an oppressed people. The very conception of true, progressive, peace-loving democracy was on trial.

3. At the bottom of the long-standing trouble between the Northern and the Southern groups of States was the North's determination to force upon the South sectionalistic legislation (centering about a so-called "protective" tariff and the exclusion of the Negro, *slave or free*,[2] from the new Western territories) and the South's determination to resist it. No God-fearing man will justify the cold-blooded assassination of Lincoln; neither should he approve the hostile and ruthless course toward the South which served as the excuse for the murder; a deliberate course of invasion, devastation, and conquest waged upon the Southern peoples despite their pleas for peace; a course which invited the penalty pronounced in the Bible (Matthew xxvi. 52) against those who take the sword.

2. See the writer's pamphlet, "Was It Anti-Slavery?" and Ewing's *Legal and Historical Status of the Dred Scott Decision*, Chapter 1.

The Washington Government's negotiations with the Confederate commissioners preceding the bombardment of Fort Sumter bore all the earmarks of trickery. "The crooked paths of diplomacy," wrote President Davis to the Confederate Congress "can scarcely furnish an example so wanting in courtesy, in candor, and in directness as was the course of the United States Government toward our commissioners in Washington."[3]

The Southern Confederacy's position was pacific in the extreme. "We protest solemnly in the face of mankind," Mr. Davis wrote in his message of April 29, 1861, to Congress, "that we desire peace at any sacrifice save that of honor and independence. We seek no conquest, no aggrandizement, no concession of any kind from the States with which we were lately confederated: all we ask is to be let alone; that those who never held power over us shall not now attempt

3. *Messages and Papers of the Confederacy*, Vol. I., p. 71. See the facts discussed at length, with verbatim communications to and from Secretary Seward, *Messages and Papers of the Confederacy*, Vol. I., pp. 82-98: also *Official Records of the War*, Series 4, Vol. I., pp. 256 *et seq.,* and Series I, Vol. LIII., pp. 161-164, and A. H. Stephens' *History of the United States*, pp. 607-609, and Appendix N

our subjugation by arms."[4] In the winter of 1860-61 Southern leaders in the Congress of the United States, Mr. Davis and Mr. Toombs among the number, advocated a constitutional amendment validating the "Missouri Compromise" line, excluding Negro slavery from the common territories north of thirty-six degrees, thirty minutes north latitude, by which the Northwest would have been left for unrestricted Northern expansion and the Southwest for Southern expansion, to the real benefit of both sections and races.[5] And the plea of the South in the "Peace Congress" of the States, winch was assembled that winter at Virginia's call, was concession and conciliation.

No fair-minded man can read the diplomatic and official record of those proceedings, especially those centering about the Confederate commission to Washington, without concluding that the Lincoln administration deliberately and successfully blocked the South's earliest efforts at conciliation and did so in order that the South might be driven to some overt act, such as the bombardment of Fort Sumter, which would inflame the still reluctant North into supporting a program of invasion and conquest and the impo-

4. *Ibid.*, p. 82.
5. Stephens, *History of the United States*, p. 569.

sition upon free and sovereign States and peoples of the shackles of government from the top.

4. Mr. Justice Campbell, of the Supreme Court of the United States, wrote to Mr. Seward, Lincoln's Secretary of State, under date of April 13, 1861: "I think no candid man who will read over what I have written and consider for a moment what is going on at Sumter but will agree that the equivocating conduct of the Lincoln administration is the proximate cause of the great calamity."[6]

The Southern States in withdrawing from the old partnership of States had acted only after careful deliberation by the peoples of the several States, each State for itself, and under explicit directions from the people to their servants, the proper public officials of the respective States. The Lincoln administration replied first by the maneuvers above noted relative to Fort Sumter, then by calling for troops to invade the South. (Several months later, when war was already actually begun, Congress was assembled.) No sovereign conventions of the people were called in the North, as was done in the South (by a sort of popular referendum) to pass upon the immediate crisis precipitated upon the country. Analogous

---

6. *Messages and Papers of the Confederacy*, Vol. I., p. 96.

to those conventions which acted upon the Federal Constitution of 1789 and accepted it, each convention acted for its own particular State. The leaders of Lincoln's party, having taken the awful responsibility, in fomenting the "free-soil" and "anti-slavery" agitation, of flounting the solemn warnings of Washington and Jefferson[7] against "geographical discriminations" – i.e. aggressive sectionalism – as inimical to continued union, now assumed the further responsibility of rebuffing the advances of the South in the Peace Congress and then actually inaugurating war by action of the executive department of the Government alone, whereas Congress, under the Constitution (Article I., Section 8), is the war-making power.

The triumph of the Confederate States would have been a notable triumph for government by the people and for peaceable adjustment of grave international or intersectional disputes. Negro slavery, for which South and North were alike responsible, eventually would have gone and with little or no bloodshed. The United States would have been no more destroyed than was the British Empire by the independence of the revolted colonies, and in the one case, as in the other, the portion remaining under the old govern-

7. Washington's Farewell Address; *The Writings of Thomas Jefferson* (1829), Vol. IV., pp. 323-4.

ment would have been actually stronger from the true democratic standpoint by reason of the lesson learned of the vital necessity of protecting the rights of a minority section. Appomattox put back the hand of progress fully half a century on the dial plate of political liberty, and the self-governing rights of smaller States or nations (real minority protection) awaited its formal recognition by the allies in the war of 1914.

If the State, simple or confederated, is conceived of as the foundation of rights and its interests are regarded as paramount to those of the constituent units, be those units individuals or commonwealths, it is only a short step to the conclusion that that State is not bound by the moral principles which are binding upon individuals.

5. The point to which such a State or nation will go in violating moral principles may depend entirely upon what the rulers at the moment in power regard as the self-interest of the State. What that self-interest is conceived at any time to be depends in turn upon the prevailing view of *national destiny.*

We know to-day what infinite suffering resulted from the Northern invasion of the seceded States. We realize how utterly impossible it always is for the ruthless invader and conqueror to make adequate amends for unspeakable loss. As we view one tragic event that succeeded another – rape following robbery and murder accompanied by devastation and political slavery – we are forcibly reminded that all this is excusable only on the specious plea of self-interest and "necessity," or military need.

6. Interstate comity and broad humanity would have been violated by the invasion and coercion of the peace-pleading Southern States even if there had been no express guaranty by treaty, Constitution, or other formal compact for the observance of the freedom and sovereignty of those commonwealths. But there was such an express guaranty. At least three of the States – Virginia, New York, and Rhode Island – in ratifying the Federal Constitution formally reserved the right of secession, or of "resumption" of the delegated powers.[8] Nor did the Constitution declare that the Union thereunder should be "perpetual," as had the old Articles of Confederation (in their title and also in Article 13) regarding the old Union, from which "perpetual Union" each of the States ratifying the new Constitution of 1789 thereupon seceded or withdrew. Moreover, a proposal to embody in the Constitution a power to coerce a recalcitrant State was opposed in the Constitutional Constitution of 1787 on the ground that this would mean war, and the proposal was

8. Elliott's *Debates*, Vol. I., pp. 327-9, 334-5.

voted clown.[9] The late Charles Francis Adams, of Massachusetts, a veteran of the Northern armies of 1861-65, has remarked that for the first forty or fifty years or so after the adoption of the Federal Constitution the ultimate right of secession, "in case of a final, unavoidable issue," was generally recognized in the North and the South alike.[10]

Now, among individuals it is, of course, elementary law and morals that a settled construction of a contract (let alone an express condition by some of the parties embodying that construction) at the time the contract is made cannot rightfully be changed thereafter when the changing interests of one or some of the parties invite such a change against the interests of others of the parties to such contract. And Mr. Pepper says that the same code of morals binds individuals and nations alike. Again, in law and in morals a contract violated in a vital particular by one or more of the parties to it is no longer binding upon the other party or parties.[11]

We have seen that the compact, or contract,

9. *Ibid.*, Vol. V., pp. 127-8, 140.

10. *Centennial Address on Robert E. Lee*, 1907, pamphlet, p. 10.

11. *American and English Encyclopedia of Law*, first edition, Vol. III., pp. 908, *et seq.*

of union between the States in 1789 was entered into in order *"to establish justice, insure domestic tranquillity, * * * and promote the general welfare."* In 1860, by a strictly sectionalist vote, an administration was elected which was pledged to keep the Southerners, with their Negroes, out of the common territories won by the common blood and treasure of South and North alike; and many prominent supporters of this new, now victorious political party had openly sympathized with John Brown in his recent efforts to incite a servile insurrection in the South, thus threatening deliberate and wholesale rapine and devastation.[12] Surely for the South under such an administration and such a party the constitutional contract was violated in most vital and essential particulars and no longer made for justice or for the South's domestic tranquillity or her general welfare.

In the face, then, of these plain, stubborn, indisputable facts of record, and in view of that rule of legal and moral conduct which is equally binding upon individuals and upon nations, there was no possible excuse for what was then perpetrated – the invasion, devastation, and conquest of the Southern States – except *the self-interest of the invaders,* real or imagined; "a process of

---

12. Stephens, *History of the United States*, p. 556; Pollard, *Lost Cause*, pp. 73, 74.

natural evolution," Charles Francis Adams calls it in his very interesting address to the University of South,[13] and this is only another way of saying "manifest destiny."

7. The issue must not be obscured by insisting that in the course of the war of 1861-65 cruelties were practiced on both sides. It is inevitable that this should be so. But the things which individuals or even nations do under provocation and in violation of their own standards are not to be compared with the outworkings of a ruthless system founded upon "manifest destiny" and logically buttressed by "military necessity." Such in the last analysis is the difference between a centralized government from the top and decentralized government by the people under written constitutions or charters of government. When seeking for historical comparisons from American annals to shame German barbarities in the war of 1914, Northern papers turned to Lee in Pennsylvania and Semmes on the sea[14] – not to Butler in New Orleans with his unspeakable Order No. 28; not to Sheridan with his torch in the Shenan-

---

13. Page 13 of the address as published (1912) in pamphlet form and entitled *The Sixty Years Since*.

14. The newspaper clippings not at present available. (As I recall it, the *New York World* and a Chicago daily are the papers in question. L.T.E.).

doah Valley nor to Sherman with his torch in Atlanta and Columbia and his deliberate depopulation of Atlanta; not to Halleck in his official suggestion that Charleston be razed and sown with salt[15]; not even to the policy adopted by Lincoln's administration by which medicine itself was made contraband of war against the beleaguered South,[16] thus condemning to wasting disease and lingering death not only countless sick or wounded soldiers, including Northern captives in Confederate prisons, but also many women and little children among those "enemies" which Scripture commands that we feed and minister unto in their distress.

Such was the natural result of training in the most insidious ways the great people of a great section of country to conceive of a supposed sectional and national self-interest as of more concern than the faithful observance of weighty contractual obligations and the solemn

---

15. *Official Records of the War*, Series 1, Vol, XV., p. 426; *ibid.*, Vol. XLIII, Part I., p. 917; *ibid.*, Vol. XLIV., p. 8; *ibid.*, *Confederate Military History*, Vol. V., pp. 365-6 (burning of Columbia); *Official Records*, Series 1, Vol. XLIV., p. 741.

16. *Congressional Record*, Vol. IV., p. 347; *Confederate Military History*, Vol., I., pp. 487, 495-6; *Confederate Veteran*, July, 1915, pp. 302-3.

warnings of the Revolutionary and constitutional-
ist fathers.

As remarked above, it is regrettable that
such issues as these should be thrust upon us in
the midst of the common struggle of South and
North against a European foe. But when the situation is thus taken advantage of to draw an attempted parallel by which the invading hosts of
the 'sixties are made to stand for the cause and
underlying principles of our present allies, and
the invaded South of the 'sixties is made to represent our ruthless enemy of to-day, we of the
South must insist on being heard in a solemn appeal to the record. God helping us, we can do no
other.

APPENDIX TWO

☆ ☆ ☆ ☆

The Causes of the War Between the States

When the smoke of the American Revolution lifted, it discovered to the world a straggling line of thirteen petty republics fringing for a thousand miles and more the western shore of the Atlantic. Only comparatively homogeneous in blood, these stripling commonwealths were varied in latitude and diversified in temperament, tendencies, and material interests. But recently brought together in one common contest against a common oppressor across the seas, harmony dwindled and discord grew between them in proportion as the late joint struggle for independence receded into the past. Grouped, regrouped, and countergrouped into large and small States, free-labor and slave-labor States, planter and sea-trading States, States with wide stretches of Western hinterland and States without, the baker's dozen of mutually jealous little Minervas eyed each other furtively from the very start.

Even during the War for Independence little Maryland held up the Articles of Confederation from unanimous adoption and actual operation until assured of a satisfactory disposition of the vast Western land grants held by Virginia and others of the large States. It appears that as early as 1786 many in the North and East favored an agreement with Spain for closing the Mississippi as a trade outlet for the scattered but growing settlements beyond the mountains. New England particularly (herself cut off from Western expansion by her geographical position) was found ever hostile to Southern and Western extensions. Bear this fact well in mind in tracing the later course of what came to be the great intersectional controversy. Again, many and significant evidences of jealousy between various States or groups of States and between the two great sections of South and North are found in the debates of the general and State conventions that framed and that adopted the Federal Constitution of 1787-89. No wonder that Washington in his farewell address considered the new Constitution and his "confederated republic" thereunder as an "experiment."

One of the "compromises of the Constitution" resulted from a "deal" between certain States of sea-trading, slave-transporting New England and some of the Southern States by which the proposed provision requiring a two-thirds vote in Congress in matters regulating commerce (including sea carriage) was defeated, and the importation of slaves from Africa should not be abolished before the year 1808.

There was pronounced opposition in New England to the purchase of the great Louisiana territory by Jefferson's administration in 1803. Like opposition from the same quarter developed some eight years later to the admission of the southernmost portion of this Louisiana country as the State of Louisiana; and Representative Josiah Quincy, of Massachusetts, uttered from the floor of Congress his famous threat of secession by "some" of the States, "amicably if they can. violently if they must."

The War of 1812 gave occasion for yet further expressions of disaffection up New England way. The Federalist party, with its stronghold there, had become hopelessly ousted from power by the Democrats, led by Jefferson and other Southern men. Moreover, the trade restrictions resulting from the war and other policies of the Democrats bore hard upon New England's sea-carrying interests, although Mr. Wilson remarks in his *History of the American People* that the planters of the South were even harder hit. In the midst of this war the memorable Hartford Convention of New Englanders was held as an angry protest against the war and the administration. This convention squinted toward secession and almost the same time Daniel Webster on the floor of the House of Representatives, speaking in opposition to one of the war measures, threatened disunion in no uncertain tones.

A few years after the war the question of Western expansion was again up. This was in 1819-21, when "the Missouri questions" shook the country from end to end. New England and the North generally opposed the admission of this new Southern and Western State. For the first time *slavery as a distinctly sectional issue* came to the fore. If the West must be settled after all, the North and the Northeast were determined to keep as much of it as possible for themselves and for White labor as against the South and Black labor. The dispute raged long and hot, involving many legislative proposals and party maneuvers.

It is very commonly supposed that the slave-labor State of Missouri and the free-labor State of Maine were together admitted under the "Missouri Compromise," by which Missouri was allowed to come in with slavery but no more slave-labor States were to be admitted from the Louisiana Purchase north of latitude thirty-six degrees, thirty minutes. This is not correct. Under such a proposal Maine was admitted; but Northern members afterwards voted against the admission of Missouri with slavery, and her admission was delayed another year.[1]

The aged Jefferson, himself an abolitionist from principle, decried this injection of politico-moral questions into intersectional politics. He said it smote upon his ears "like a fire bell in the night" and could mean only bloodshed and disunion. Jefferson pointed out that true friends of the Negroes should be glad to see them diffused over a larger stretch of country. That this "anti-slavery" stand of the North in Congress was economic and political, not moral and philanthropic, is manifest from a study of the laws of those times in Northern and Northwestern States aimed against free Negroes there.

For a few years after the admission of Missouri the question of Western expansion as a sectional issue slept, then broke forth again at the time of the nullification crisis, 1830-33. Senator Foot, of Connecticut, had introduced a resolution looking to the restriction of the survey and sale of Western lands. The South and the West attacked it as designed to retard the development

---

1. See the history of this most informingly discussed in A.H. Stephens's *History of the United States*.

of the West and to keep the factory laborers of the North from emigrating. Too, the moneyed interests (centered in the North) were accused of wishing to maintain a permanent, interest-bearing national debt. Manufactures had received a great impetus during the trade troubles accompanying the second war with Britain, and "protective" tariffs had been demanded by and conceded to the manufacturers. These were mostly in the middle States, but by 1830 were quite numerous in New England also.

By her determined stand in the nullification crisis, South Carolina, reënforced by widespread sympathy in other Southern States, forced a radical reduction in the tariff under the famous compromise of 1833. She thereby incurred the lasting enmity of New England and of much of the North generally. Up to this date the abolitionist crusade had made no great headway in the North, least of all in New England. But it was in the midst of these nullification debates in Congress that John Quincy Adams uttered the significant threat that if "protection" of manufacturers was not to be given to the North, then the South ought not to expect continued protection of Negro slavery. It was from this very juncture that abolitionism and "free-soilism" began to make marked growth throughout the North. Except for a brief period in the early 'forties, a low or lowered tariff prevailed from nullification until the war of 1861.

In the nullification debates we find the agricultural South and West, for the most part, standing together against the common hostility of the mercantile North and East. But a change soon took place. The North found that the West was bound to grow, anyhow. Largely increased immigration from Europe began about this time to pour into Northern ports and to furnish the needed cheap labor for Northern mills; the West was steadily beguiled with the prospect of vast "internal improvements" (roads, aids to navigation, etc.), at the expense of the Federal treasury. These improvements called for large revenue and so lent added plausibility to the demand for a high tariff on imports. Thus, long before 1861 the Northeast and the Northwest became allied against the South. But few Europeans came into the South, where the immigrant laborers would find themselves in competition with slave labor. Thus the North's population grew faster than the South's. Also these Continental Europeans were imbued with the ideas of strong monarchical, centralistic governments, and so were the more ready to embark upon a war of invasion and conquest (when the issue with the South should once be finally drawn) and thus help overwhelm the minority, though a considerable one, in the North opposed to any such repudiation of the principles of our Declaration of Independence and our historical, constitutional rights. Lincoln in his war of coercion derived much aid and comfort from the German immigrants with their ideals of blood and iron.

Meanwhile many in the North had opposed the annexation of Texas, also that of other Southwestern territory, resulting from the war with Mexico. The Kansas-Nebraska controversy gave rise to the Republican party in the 'fifties, which demanded that the South keep out of the common territories which had been acquired by the common blood and treasure of the South and North alike. Horace Greeley, one of the Republican leaders, was slow to be drawn into the professed antislavery agitation, because, as he himself said in 1845, he found too much slavery in the North. In the factory districts there the women and children toiled thirteen and fourteen hours a day, and the factory hands dwelt in the company's houses and worshiped God at the company's church.

The new party in its first national platform (1856) did not declare for a high or "protective" tariff. It polled a good vote that year and, thereby encouraged, declared for such a tariff in 1860, thus appealing to both the land-hungry of the West and the bounty-hungry of the East. Meanwhile the John Brown raid into Virginia, seeking to incite the Negroes to war with the

Southern Whites, had occurred in 1859, and widespread sympathy with and for him was expressed in the North, a sympathy doubtless fanned by Harriet Beecher Stowe's stirring novel, *Uncle Tom's Cabin*, of this period. The Democrats and the Constitutionalist-Union men split into three tickets in 1860, thus allowing the Republicans to elect their candidate by a majority of the electoral votes, though by a minority of nearly a million of the popular vote.

Most of the Southern States then withdrew, and the war of coercion followed A high tariff was promptly enacted as a "war measure" to raise revenue for waging war on the South, which was to be retained in the Union *inter alia* to furnish cheap raw materials for Northern manufacturers and perhaps an outlet for the Northwest via the Mississippi. This tariff was repeatedly increased during the four years of war. Yet, despite this need of revenue, the free-homestead act of 1862 was passed, thus materially reducing the income from the disposal of the new lands of the West. And with it all a huge public debt was piled up.

Some one has aptly remarked that the Northern writers have been too prone to ascribe moral causes to the great war of the 'sixties and Southern writers too much inclined to lay it to a difference of view of constitutional rights; that, in truth, the causes were primarily economic. Commercial and economic questions have caused most of the great wars of history, and human nature is the same in America as elsewhere. In his farewell address Washington warned against belief in disinterested kindness in national conduct; Mr. Taft has spoken to like effect. Tariff, Western lands, immigration, the desire in certain selfishly interested quarters for a big permanent public debt – all these had more to do with our great war than the historians have usually told us.

APPENDIX THREE

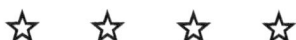

☆ ☆ ☆ ☆

Slavery and Wage Serfdom

On February 21, 1821, William Brown, member of the House of Representatives from Kentucky, moved a resolution looking to the formal repeal of the "Missouri Compromise" of the preceding year, on the ground that faith had been broken by the North in rejecting Missouri after the passage of the compromise and because of the prospect of the North's continued rejection of her admission as a State.

In his speech in Congress the same day supporting this resolution Mr. Brown said some things worthy of preservation in the chronicles of those times and as pertinent to the general subject of the intersectional questions of 1819-61. Not only did Brown, like Thomas Jefferson, urge that the diffusion of the Negroes over a wider area by the admission of such new border

States as Missouri would not add to the number of slaves; he argued further that such dispersion among a proportionately larger White population would tend "further to increase the prospects for manumission by masters and gradual abolition by the State governments."

Turning to another phase of the controversy, Mr. Brown said:

"Sir, a venerable and distinguished Senator from New York (Mr. King) said when speaking of the slaveholding States that in them 'manual labor dishonored the hands of freemen. And the same sentiment has been reëchoed in this House. I deny the proposition to be true and can and now will proceed to show that this is not one of the evils of African slavery, but that its existence in a society elevates the poor and laboring white man and that its nonexistence invites and leads to his depression and dishonor. Sir, where slavery is tolerated slaves perform for others the servile and menial duties of the stable, the kitchen, and the house; * * * the whites engage in the dignified and honorable labor of agriculture and the mechanic arts, and in these respectable men and their sons, slaveholders and non-slaveholders, indiscriminately join. * * * When, sir, in the State which I have in part the honor to represent a man in the higher walks of life meets his poor but honest neighbor, he salutes him and treats him with the attention which belongs to merit. If he comes to his house, he is met at the door and cordially taken by the hand, invited to a seat in the hospitable circle, and constitutes a welcome guest at the smoking board. But what is the picture in the nonslaveholding States? I speak the language of experience and truth. The wealthy employ, I do not say culpably, the poor and miserable whites in all the round of servile duties from the stable to the kitchen; they ride before and behind their carriages and stand often trembling in the presence of their august employers, in practice and truth their masters; they act as their cook, their shoeblacks. and their scullions. The wide chasm between their stations and pursuits forbids intercourse at all, much less a cordial one. * * * Since the days of Adam to the present time men have occupied the various stations of high and low, rich and poor, dignified and servile, and the practical difference betwixt the slaveholding and the nonslaveholding States upon this subject is that the former have degraded their black and the latter their white brethren to those servile duties."

Very possibly this was an overdrawn picture by the representative from slaveholding Kentucky. But it is worth preserving alongside and comparing with the many dark delineations at Northern hands of the downtrodden condition in the South of all persons outside the favored few of the actual slaveholders; worth, too, bearing in mind in connection with what we can readily ascertain of the condition of factory labor in the ante-bellum North. Thus in 1835 the workmen *lost a general strike for the ten-hour day* throughout the Boston district, as we are reminded by Mr. John R. Commons, of the University of Wisconsin, in his thoughtful brochure, "Horace Greeley and the Working Class Origin of the Republican Party."

The condition of the laboring classes of New England way was indeed pitiable. In such condition Daniel Webster at this time could have found, had he been so minded, vindication for his stand of an earlier time in his career when he had declared:

"I am not anxious to accelerate the approach of the period when the great mass of American labor shall not find its employment in the field, when the young men of the country shall be obliged to shut their eyes upon external nature, upon the heavens and the earth, and immerse themselves in close and unwholesome workshops. * * * It is the true policy of government to suffer the different pursuits of society to take their own course and not to give excessive bounties or encouragements to one over another. This also is the true spirit of the Constitution."

Moreover, Mr. Webster would have found that his "young men" were not the only or the frailest victims.

Mr. Commons further tells us:

"Meanwhile the factory system had grown up at Lowell and other places, with its *women and children on duty thirteen and fourteen hours a day,* living in company houses, eating at the company table, and required to attend the company church. While some of the ten-hour strikes of 1833 had been successful in Philadelphia and in New York, the working people of New England were doomed to the long day for another fifteen years."

Under such conditions as these no wonder that the bighearted Greeley, as quoted by Mr. Commons, wrote as follows to the Anti-Slavery Convention at Cincinnati in 1845:

"If I am less troubled concerning the slavery prevalent in Charleston or New Orleans, it is because I see so much slavery in New York which appears to claim my first efforts. * * * Wherever opportunity to labor is obtained with difficulty and is so deficient that the employing class may virtually prescribe their own terms and pay the laborer only such share at they choose of the product, there is a very strong tendency to slavery."

And if we delve a little deeper into those

times, we shall find that these tariff-nurtured, serf-driving manufacturing barons of the North had much to do with shaping the events that brought on the war of 1861 – a war that foisted and fastened upon the people a high tariff and a huge national debt. The tariff furnished wealth to the barons; the debt afforded an opportunity to invest the surplus portion of such wealth in gilt-edge securities with interest thereon guaranteed from the taxpayers at large; further, the bigger the debt, the greater the excuse for a high tariff as a means of raising revenue for the government's needs. And this shows us the vicious circle, the crushing endless chain drawn and manipulated by "big business" standing at the right hand of a strong, centralized government.

APPENDIX FOUR

☆ ☆ ☆ ☆

Abolition, Slavery, and the Year 1833

In the *Confederate Veteran* for April, 1921, we find in one of Dr. McNeill's splendid articles on Confederate history the copy of a letter to him from Dr. Albert B. Hart, historian and Northerner. The immediate subject of discussion here is "slavery," and we find Dr. Hart, Northerner, with no word of apology or regret for the orgy of invasion, conquest, bloodshed, and devastation in the course of which Negro slavery in the South was *incidentally* overthrown. He voices his shocked regret that "not one single State between 1833 and 1861 made enactments for the correction of manifest and public abuses" and because "not a single Southern State took or dared take any steps toward the education of the slave."

That slavery was indeed merely an incident of the great intersectional quarrel which culminated in the war of 1861 Dr. Hart's past writings themselves help to show. But to begin a brief discussion here of the particular point raised in the above quotations from the learned Doctor let us quote from an earlier writer – viz., Thomas Jefferson. Relative to the fierce controversy over the admission of Missouri as a State Jefferson on April 22, 1820, wrote in truly prophetic vein to the Northern Democratic leader, Holmes:

"But this momentous question, like a fire bell in the night, awakened and filled me with terror. I considered it at once *as the knell of the Union.* It is hushed indeed for the moment. But this is a reprieve only, not a final sentence. *A geographical line coinciding with a marked principle, moral and political, once conceived and held up to the angry passions of men will never be obliterated,* and every new irritation will mark it deeper and deeper. * * * The cession of that kind of property [slaves], for so it is misnamed, is a bagatelle which would not cost me a second thought if in that way a general emancipation and *expatriation* [emphasis in the original] could be effected. * * * Of one thing I am certain, that as the passage of slaves from one State to another would not make a slave of a single human being who would not be so with-out it, so their diffusion over a greater surface would make them individually happier and proportionally facilitate the accomplishment of their emancipation by dividing the burthen on a greater number of coadjutors. * * * I regret that I am now to die in the belief that the useless sacrifice of themselves by the generation of 1776 to acquire self-government and happiness to the country is to be thrown away by the unwise and unworthy passions of their sons and that my only consolation is to be that I live not to weep over it."

Jefferson was eternally right in deprecating a political division along geographical or sectional lines. The agitation over Missouri was a prelude to the war of 1861, which in truth destroyed *the* Union of the fathers and erected in its stead something very different.

The formative and transformative period for American Political parties and American geographical sections that had begun with the War of 1812 was well rounded out during this decade of 1820-30. By 1830 New England, the North generally, and the then Northwest are found pretty solidly lined up for a high tariff "protecting" manufactures and for a strong central government as the best favoring such paternalistic legislation; the agricultural, slave-labor South against such.

Now, before 1830 abolition as a cause or propaganda and aside from its growing political aspect was of a distinctly mild and nonsectionalist type compared with its later history. In Dr.

Hart's book, *Slavery and Abolition*, we read that in the decade of the 'twenties "the hostility to slavery became a distinct propaganda which took on three different forms: an attempt through Churches and other existing means to arouse public sentiment, an organized emancipation agitation directed by a national society, and colonization. Unlike later abolition, this whole movement was carried on *by people who lived in or adjoining slaveholding States.*" It was in this decade, according to Dr. Hart, that the earlier and milder abolitionism reached its full growth and began to decline. "When Jackson became President [1829]," says the Doctor (page 165), "antislavery seemed, after fifty years of effort, to have spent its force. The voice of the Churches was no longer heard in protest; the abolitionist societies were dying out; there was hardly an abolitionist militant in the field: the colonization society absorbed most of the public interest in the subject, and it was doing nothing to help either the free negro or the slave: in Congress there was only one antislavery man, and his efforts were without avail."

The question arises, Why this decline in the antislavery sentiment at this time as thus depicted circumstantially by Dr. Hart?

By way of a summary statement of political affairs at this juncture: The year 1830 found the question of new Western States (which had involved a crisis over the admission of Missouri, 1819-21) as a sectional issue between North and South, no longer to the front for pressing present settlement, but bound to recur in the future; "protectionist" sentiment, having overspread the whole North (New England last of all), was regarded as firmly established in national legislation, but was beginning to lose its grip at least on the masses of the people as distinguished from the manufacturers in the Northern States; antislavery was at ebb tide throughout the border States and in the North, while as yet it had at no time made any considerable headway in New England even when strongest elsewhere. Mark well each of the several sets of facts summarized in this paragraph and bear in mind their *respective situations* at this juncture of affairs before we take up the ensuing developments.

Just at this time came a great political crisis, the nullification episode of the early 'thirties (a most interesting and informing chapter in itself). The outcome of this nullificationist clash is well known – South Carolina and the cause of a *constitutional* revenue tariff triumphed, but not until the United States had been brought to the brink of war among themselves. The compromise tariff act of 1833, a direct result of South Carolina's bold stand, scaled down the customs duties, although by easy stages, to a revenue basis.

Big was the wrath and consternation of the high "protection" advocates. Introduced as the measure was by Henry Clay, the great high priest of "protection" and of the "American system," Clay's defection was likened by *Niles's Register,* a "protectionist" organ, to "a crash of thunder in the winter season."

Dr. Hart in the book above mentioned remarks (chapter 12) on the prevailing apathy in the North about 1830 on the subject of abolition and asks: "Why did the antislavery movement, which had been going on steadily for half a century, apparently die down in 1829 and then suddenly blaze up with renewed fierceness?" The Doctor then essays to answer his own question. But, after thus arousing the curiosity of his readers by this pointed and pertinent query, he proves rather disappointingly short on assigned causes. "One reason" he finds in the fact that "the Western world was growing tired of human bondage, the last vestige of serfdom was disappearing in Central Europe, and the same spirit extended to the European colonies in America" He says further that "slavery was also unfavorably affected by the sudden opening up of new fields of economic activity. The development of manufactures, the growth of large cities, and the exchange of products far and wide called for *a kind of laborer who instinctively felt that the slave was a competitor.*" Very good, Doctor: but all in all scarcely a full and satisfactory explanation for both the general falling to pieces of an ancient agitation and then the sudden rehabilitation of the same, although the words we here put in italics are of considerable significance.

So let us take up the inquiry at this point. By 1830 a "protective" tariff, theretofore of gen eral popularity in the North after once the sentiment there for it had grown, had become apparently a permanency in Federal legislation. But immediately thereafter, just as the tariff-nurtured barons were saying, "Peace and safety," sudden destruction came upon them in the shape of Clay's compromise tariff of 1833, to them the bitter fruit of South Carolina's resolute course.

Now, mark this: in the midst of the debates in Congress, A.D. 1833, over nullification John Quincy Adams, of Massachusetts, ex-President and now in the House of Representatives, uttered this highly portentous language:

"Well, if they must withdraw protection from the free white labor of the North, then it ought to be withdrawn from the machinery [slave labor] of the South. Let them disband their [the United States] army; this would go as far as four or five millions toward reducing the revenue to the wants of the government. The next step was to abolish the navy, for why commerce and navigation continue to enjoy protection when it was withdrawn from other interests of the country? Well, when this had been done and Congress had been so very generous as to give away all the public lands, what, he asked, would remain for the general government to do? Nothing. There would be nothing for it to do. * * * No government would be needed. Let it go back to its original elements, let it go back to the States, let it go back to the Confederation – go back to the people. This was the legitimate consequence of those arguments urged by gentlemen who would no longer submit to a system of [customs] protection."

Before this time Mr. Adams, according to Dr. Hart, had never been noted for his active antislavery sympathies; rather the reverse. And he reviews Adams's record in this regard. But now simultaneously with South Carolina's triumphant check to Northern "protectionism" and with "protectionist" Adams's appearance as an active antislavery champion in the halls of Congress began a new chapter of antislavery agitation in what was now firmly "protectionist" New England. We learn from Dr. Hart that about this time *abolition* and *antislavery* in the North approach a coalition; that "political abolitionists" now first make their appearance. He tells us that New England was "still inactive" in the cause as late as 1832. Now, 1832 was the year *before* Mr. Clay's bolt from the "protectionist" reservation and the resultant thunderbolt from the blue. But soon, presto! we learn from the same authority that "outside of New England" gradual emancipation, as distinguished from ceaseless agitation for immediate and complete abolition, was acceptable with the agitators.

And as typical of his native New England in this respect, Adams, now that at last he had got to going strong, kept up the pace. On May 23, 1836, in an extended speech he predicted Congressional interference in case of a general slave insurrection. In 1842, April 14, Adams declared in Congress that "when a country is invaded and two hostile armies are set in hostile array the commanders of both armies have power to emancipate all the slaves in the invaded territory – which last speech, according to his own gloating comment, "stung the slavocracy [sic] to madness." Yes, once enlisted in the "antislavery," anti-Southern cause, New England appears to have speedily overtaken and passed the earlier starting Middle Atlantic and Ohio-Valley North. And forget not that these were, from the "protectionist" standpoint, the beginning of the lean years under a reduced tariff.

The year 1833, then, checked in the interest

of the South the tariff-fed exploiters at the North. The year 1833 marks the beginning of the new abolitionist drive by Northerners, with John Quincy Adams as one of the most aggressive leaders. Active agitation of this sort threatened, of course, the "servile insurrections" deprecated in the Declaration of Independence and exemplified in the Nat Turner uprising this very period and in the John Brown raid of some twenty five years later. Is it any wonder that from 1833, as mentioned by Dr. Hart in his letter to Dr. McNeilly, there was cessation in the South of remedial legislation in behalf the slaves?

In the sharp clash between the South and North over conflicting economic interests during the four decades preceding the war for Southern independence the poor negro was merely a stalking horse or a pawn on the chess board. The fervor of a few hottest fanatics was turned to good account by the "practical" leaders in the North, who knew just what they wanted in the matter of tariffs, public lands to be settled by whites alone, etc. Yea, verily the whole story of "abolitionist" and "antislavery" agitation in the Northern States is merely another chapter in the long, sinister story of cant and hypocrisy on the part of white races in dealing with alien and backward peoples of darker skins – exploitation of the weak by the strong.

But were was this difference: The North, for its own selfish, material interests, for the sake of obtaining favors in the way of Congressional legislation and at the expense of the South, further complicated an already delicate interracial situation. The South, facing a condition rather than a theory, was driven to the defense of her home and hearthstone under nature's first law, that of self-preservation. So Dr. Hart in his letter to Dr. McNeilly has been already answered by the stubborn facts of history set forth in large part by Dr. Hart's own book. But Dr. A. W. Littlefield, of Massachustts, hits the bull's-eye when he declares that with the radical differences of interest in those times in the matter of a tariff between the South and North a great war between them was bound to come, even had there never been a slave in the Southland.

APPENDIX FIVE

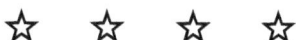

☆　☆　☆　☆

Builder and Defacer

I. Jefferson

Young Jefferson, aristocrat by birth,
Looked forth on fertile fields and fair – his own;
Both wealth and culture his. At his command
All that might go to make a life of ease
Such life as oft doth dull one's sympathies
For fellow man whose lot is rougher cast.

But better, stouter stuff than this was he;
lie soared above such weak and sordid souls.
Beneath the Southland's soft blue, sunny skies,
Virginia's verdant vales all voiced in him:
"Live and let live. Or high or low degree,
Man is my brother still. Life, liberty,
Pursuit of happiness, are his as mine;
And stanch should stand as yonder
Blue Ridge rests."

Nor did he stop with thoughts or words that give
The boon of hope to ear but break the heart;
Deep in the statute law he wrote his rules,
That his fair land, America, might prove
For freemen all a home of equal rights,
And privilege be shorn of place and power.[1]

Thus through his lengthened life did Jefferson
Make good the promise of his early pen:
First, for these struggling peoples he declared
Their right to rule themselves,
though kings might frown.
Such right for other freemen, too, wherever they;
Then, freedom won, he fashioned fair for all,
That clue nor class might claim the land as theirs.

He even planned that freedom's boon might come
To th' alien race of bondmen in our midst –
But in a home and land their very own;
And sternly warned that section's faction rest,
Nor bathe the land in blood on such false plea.
He planned: but only one life's span was his;
Such work were great, the road so very long.[2]

---

1. "A home of equal rights," etc. Jefferson is generally recognized as having done much, in drafting the Declaration of Independence, in the legislation he helped enact and in promulgating the principles of the great political party he founded, to put in force his own slogan: "Equal rights for all, special privileges for none."

2. Jefferson and the Negro. Thomas Jefferson favored emancipation of the slaves (by State action) and their "ex-

Thus Jefferson. We make not him a god,
Nor perfect man; for faults were his enow.
His fame needs bolster none as this would be.
Suffice that he, a man of clay, like us,
Stands on his merits with posterity
As one who deeply drank at Freedom's fount,
And pointed true for myriads yet unborn
The road of statecraft, home rule, right, and peace.

II. Lincoln

In Jefferson's declining years, it fell
One saw the light of day in frontier wilds –
A yeoman man child on Kentucky's shore.
Young Lincoln grew as grew the lads about:
Scant store of life's good things was his; but see,
Youth, health, he had, and much of energy.

Virginia's child, Kentucky; thence went he
To Illinois, the land Virginia gave
To South and North alike by wresting it

---

patriation" (deportation or emigration to another country).
He opposed the beginnings of the sectionalist abolition or
"free-soil" movement, comparing the "Missouri question"
(1819-21) to a "fire bell in the night," that portended
bloodshed between North and South, overthrow of the
constitutional union of the States, and the undoing of the
work of 1776. (See, *inter al.,* his letter of April 22, 1820,
to Holmes, Volume IV. of his writings, 1829 edition., pp.
323-4, cited also "(Stephens' *History of the United States*,
p. 431) as in Volume VII. of his *Complete Works*, p. 159.)

From foemen's hands in far-off wilderness,
While yet we battled on Atlantic's slope
For right to range ourselves 'mong nations free.
And here he wrought right lustily: the years
Were kind; and so a place and name he made.[3]

Well, time went on. Then, hot and hotter still,
Raged strife of sections for the bounding West.
Or slave or free, the Negro, none of him
Did Northrons wish in these new lands; for see
The laws they wrote to keep him out. And then,
Of trade and tariffs there was quarrel, too.[4]

Unheeded now dead Jefferson: the rift
Had come. And clique and class now cloked amain
With cunning rare, and wage serfs made the while
They cried aloud of Southland's slavery sin.
And Lincoln rode the tide. By section's vote
They placed him in the chair of state, to rule
O'er South and North – as Northland
might decree.[5]

---

3. Virginia sent George Rogers Clarke, during the Revolutionary War, on the daring expedition that won the trans-Ohio country from the British.

4. Laws to exclude free Negroes from the North and Northwest. (See *inter al.,* Ewing's *Legal and Historical Status of the Dred Scott Decision*, chapter 4.)

5. "Wage serfs, "etc. Horace Greeley, as late as 1845, expressed lack of enthusiasm for the then professed anti-slavery agitation, because, he said, he saw so much of slavery in the factory districts of the North. (See the two

Then spake the South: "In peace now let us part."
Great-hearted Greeley grieved, but said "Amen!"
Some asked "Whence come our revenues and gains,
    If thus they go?" And Lincoln, heeding these,
    First warred as might a king – and *later* called
That Congress meet. How strange! And thus we see
    This plain man from the mass so mar the shrine
    Of Freedom fair reared high by Jefferson.[6]

And class and clique from that day on have ruled,
    And equal rights gone down – a thing of scorn.
    And superman, or demigod, they make
    In memory now of him who wrought for them:

---

pamphlets, Commons's "Working Class Origin of the
Republican Party," and Everett's "Was It Anti-Slavery?"
6. "Greeley . . . said, 'Amen!" After the election of Lincoln,
by a strictly sectionalist vote, in 1860, Horace Greeley's
paper, the *New York Tribune* (Nov. 26, 1860, and Dec. 17,
1860, as quoted in Pollard's *Lost Cause*, pp. 84-5), organ
of Lincoln's party though it was, insisted that the "Cotton
States," if they so wished, be left to secede in peace, and
decried a union "whereof one section is pinned to the residue
by bayonets." "Whence come our revenues and gains?"
The tariff barons of the North were interested in keeping
the agricultural South for exploitation purposes, under the
same government with themselves, in this much like certain
commercial interests of Britain during the American
Revolution. "First warred as might a king," etc. In April,
1861, Lincoln began war on the Confederate States by
attempting to strengthen his hold on Fort Sumter by calling
out troops, etc. He did not convene Congress until July.

Lincoln, the weakest link in empire's chain
How careful they to gild all mere alloy![7]

III. Time's Test

But Truth and hope live on; and, slow but sure,
Shall facts come forth to face the future day.
Already, see how, when the World War raged,
When at the North, to shame the Hun's dark deeds,
Harked back to Lee on land, Semmes on the sea –
Not Lincoln's war lords waging Lincoln's war.
The work of Jefferson was not torn down for aye:
His mem'ry yet means much for mortal men.[8]

---

7. "Class and clique . . . have ruled," etc. From the war of 1861 on, multi-millionaires, along with tramps, have been made in America in increasing numbers. Sinister "special-interest legislation" has had much to do with this. "Lincoln, the weakest link," etc. A familiar proverb says, "The strength of a chain is its weakest link," an obvious truth. Lincoln did not "save the Union," the fathers' constitutional union of choice. He helped to destroy it, then to erect a blood-red union of force on its ruins. The whole cause of the North must stand or fall with Lincoln's unconstitutional course.

7. "Men at the North," etc. During the World War Theodore Roosevelt contrasted the ruthless sea warfare of the Germans with the humanity of Admiral Raphael Semmes, C. S. N. The *New York World* cited Lee's scrupulously humane course in Pennsylvania as against the ferocity of the German armies. They did not turn to Lincoln's lieutenants, Sherman in Georgia, Butler in New Orleans, or Sheridan and Hunter in the Valley of Virginia.